791.53 Paludan, Lis.
        Playing with puppets / Lis Paludan ;
        translated [from the Danish] by Chris-
        tine Crowley. London : Mills and Boon,
        1974.
        144 p. : ill. (some col.) ;

        Translation of Bornenes dukketeaterbog.
        Imprint covered by label which reads:
        Plays, Inc. Publishers, Boston. Illus-
        trated instructions for making various
        kinds of puppets, creating scenery, and
        putting on plays.

        1.Puppets and puppet-plays-Juv. lit.
        2.Puppets and   puppet-plays. I.Title
                                        75-318168

PLAYING WITH PUPPETS

By the same author
EASY EMBROIDERY

Playing
with Puppets

Lis Paludan

Translated by Christine Crowley

MILLS & BOON

First published as Børnenes dukketeaterbog by Bramsen &
Hjort, Copenhagen, 1972
© this edition Mills & Boon Limited, 1974

Drawings and models designed by the author
Photographs: Jes Buusmann
Translated by: Christine Crowley
Colour reproduction: Dystan, Copenhagen

ISBN 0 263 05465 9

Made & Printed in Great Britain by William Clowes & Sons,
Limited, London, Beccles and Colchester

Contents

You can make many different kinds of puppets and theatres from all sorts of material. Some of the things suggested in this book are rather difficult to make, but perhaps you can ask someone to help you. It can be great fun to have several people working together, and you will find that making the puppets and the theatre is as much fun as playing with them.

You can put a lot of effort into making splendid puppets and a very fine theatre that will give you pleasure for a long time. You can also make exciting puppets and a theatre quickly with inexpensive materials. Hunt around the house and you will find many things that can be used for theatre puppets: wooden spoons, brooms, mops, tools, and even old hats. With these articles you can easily put on a play and you can start right away!

a couple of times. Dilute the paints with a little water before you use them. Don't apply the paint too thickly or a crust will form that cracks when you move your fingers. You can also dress your hands, paint them and use two fingers of each hand as puppet legs, as in the top drawing.

Sock, glove and hat puppets

Look at the picture in the top right-hand corner on the opposite page, and the one on page 7. Here are some creatures made of old socks, gloves and hats. It is quite easy: put a sock or glove on your hand, decorate it a little, and you have a figure to play-act with. If your hand does not fill out the figure enough, put kapok in the necessary places.

The dog on page 7 has velvet eyes and ears. The man with the pipe has woollen hair and glass eyes. The red animal on page 9 is a sock with a splendid mane of frayed yarn. The strange puppet next to it is made by putting a glove on one hand and placing a beret over it. The eyes are pieces of felt with buttons sewn in the centre.

To make a sock puppet move its mouth, stuff a corner of the sock between your thumb and palm, and move your fingers. It can "speak", hold things in its mouth, and look as if it is eating.

Painted hands and feet

You can make the simplest puppets by painting your hands — or your feet. Here are some suggestions for the many funny characters you can make in this way.

Colour your hands or feet with poster paints or finger paints, which can be washed off afterwards. The red colours can be a little difficult to remove and you may have to wash

The heads in the bottom picture are made from polystyrene balls. Instructions are on pages 16 (heads) and 30 (bodies).

Finger puppets

You can make tiny puppets to fit on your fingers. Wear a glove and put the heads on the fingertips. You can make little costumes from cardboard tubes, as in the top drawing.

The puppets in the picture on the left have heads made from polystyrene balls. You can read about this on page 16. How to make a neck from a cardboard tube is explained on page 18. The puppets' hair is melted plastic straws. Stick a plastic straw into a candle flame. When it is about to melt, rub it on the puppet's head, where it will harden and stick. The costumes are pieces of fabric glued round the cardboard neck. For the arms, stick a piece of felt across the back of the costume, as in the bottom drawing.

The big white ghost is worked with the whole hand. The index finger sticks up into the head, the thumb into one arm, and the other fingers into the other arm. The middle drawing shows you how to make a pattern for the costume. Draw an outline of your hand on a piece of paper, leaving a large space between the index and other fingers. Do not draw too close to the fingers. Cut out the pattern in two pieces of fabric. Sew them together, leaving the neck and bottom open. Fix the costume to the puppet's neck neatly with a piece of adhesive tape.

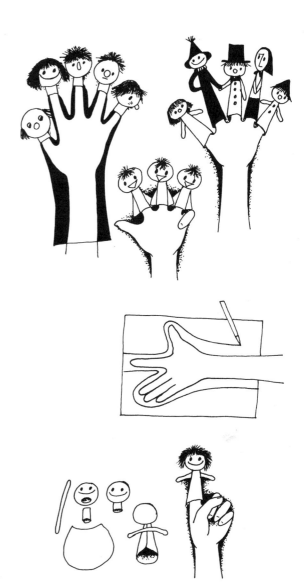

11

Heads

The head is a very important part of a puppet. Together with the costume, movements and voice you give the puppet, it must express the puppet's personality.

Make the head as simple as possible. The puppet has to be seen at a distance, and small details will simply disappear.

Unless you really must have a grinning or very sad person in your play, it is best to let the puppet's face have a neutral expression — a couple of dark dots for eyes is often enough. In this way you can express the puppet's moods by voice and movements, and use the same puppet for several different parts.

The heads can be made from almost anything — from paper bags and potatoes to papier mâché and polystyrene balls. The following pages show you how to make heads from these and other materials.

Some heads are more lasting than others. Therefore, before you start, decide whether you want to make a puppet that can be used for only one performance or one that can be used again and again.

It is best to have a stand for making heads; page 22 shows you how to make one.

Paper bag and plate-lipped puppets

Use a paper bag with a flat bottom to make a funny puppet that can move its mouth. The plate-lipped animal can move its mouth too. It is made from a sock and a bent paper plate. Decorate the puppets any way you wish — here we used parts of an egg tray for the eyes.

Using newspaper and old tights

Crumple some newspaper into a ball and glue it to the top of a cardboard tube that fits over your finger. Wind yarn round the ball to make it firm. Put a layer of kapok round it. Slip an old tights' leg over it. Page 15 shows you how to make the nose. Gather the ends of the tights' leg and sew them to the back of the head. Sew or glue on eyes and hair.

Spoon puppets

Old wooden spoons can be used as puppet heads. Glue on wool for hair and paint a face with a felt-tip pen or water colours. If you paint a sad face on one side of the spoon and a happy face on the other, you can make the puppet change expression during a play by quickly turning the spoon.

Make a costume from any fabric. Sew it on a cone shape and glue it to the neck.

Sock head

Cut off the toe section of an old sock and run a draw thread round the open end. Fill the sock with cottonwool or other stuffing. Push a cardboard tube neck into the sock. Pull the draw thread tight round the tube and tie securely. Use glue to make it more secure. Sew or glue on eyes, nose, mouth and hair.

Cardboard tube heads

It is easy to make funny heads from cardboard tubes. Find a tube that fits your three middle fingers, or make one from a piece of cardboard. It need not be the same width at both ends. Make a costume that fits your hand or use a glove.

Heads from old vests

Cut out a large circle from an old vest, blouse, etc. Run a draw thread round the edge, as shown in the drawing. To make a nose, run another draw thread round a smaller circle in the centre. Place a small ball of kapok in the inner circle, pull the draw thread round it, and tie securely.

Make a cardboard tube that fits your finger, with a rim at the top and bottom (see page 18). Pull the draw thread so that the material is half-gathered together. Now push in the stuffing. Push the cardboard tube part way into the head. Gather the fabric tightly round the top rim. Sew or glue on hair, eyes, ears and mouth.

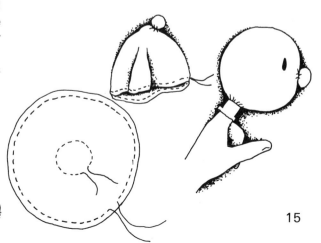

Using polystyrene balls

Polystyrene balls are available in many sizes (see page 144), and are very good for making puppet heads. They may be used as they are or as a basis for really strong puppet heads. Here are some methods.

Shaping polystyrene by melting

Polystyrene balls melt at quite low temperatures. Use an awl heated over a candle to melt holes for the neck and eyes, and a groove for the mouth. In the top drawing half a cork has been used as a nose. It is fixed on with pins; it can also be glued on. With polystyrene use only a water-based adhesive or polystyrene cement (see page 144). Never use a spirit-based adhesive on either polystyrene or foam rubber.

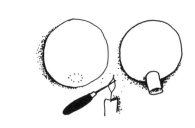

The head can be painted with acrylic or poster paints. If the poster paint does not stick, mix a little household glue into it. For hair, use wool, raffia, etc.

Cut-out polystyrene heads

Polystyrene balls can be sawn or cut. In the drawing the professor's head itself is not cut, but his nose is cut out of a smaller ball. When cut to shape, smooth the nose with sandpaper and glue it on. Make a hole for the neck tube with a hot awl. Glue on the neck tube. Paint the head and nose.

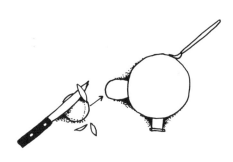

The professor's eyes are made from buttons, and the spectacles from steel wire. His hair and beard are frayed yarn, which is glued on. There is a photograph of the professor on page 85. The puppets on page 84 are made in the same way.

Polystyrene balls as basic shapes

For really fine, strong heads, use polystyrene balls as a base and glue on newspaper. Cut the ball to the shape you want. Smooth it with sandpaper and make a hole for the neck tube with a heated awl. Glue on the neck tube. Now paste on many layers of newspaper strips. To make sure that all surfaces are covered with each layer, use typing paper for every other layer. Make the nose by rolling up a paper ball and gluing it on.

When there are enough layers and the head is the shape you want, it must dry; this may take a few days. When it is completely dry, smooth it with fine sandpaper and paint it. To make the paint more lasting, spray it with a fixative when dry. The eyes can be made of Plasticine or buttons. Felt eyebrows can be glued on.

The figures in the photograph on page 91 are made in this way.

Papier mâché

Strips of newspaper pasted on in layers is called papier mâché. You can make papier mâché heads, hands, animals, shoes, sets for the theatre, and many other things. The basic form can be a polystyrene ball, a folded newspaper, a wire net, a blown-up balloon, or other things that can help you to get the shape you want. Use cold water paste, which is available as a powder, when making papier mâché.

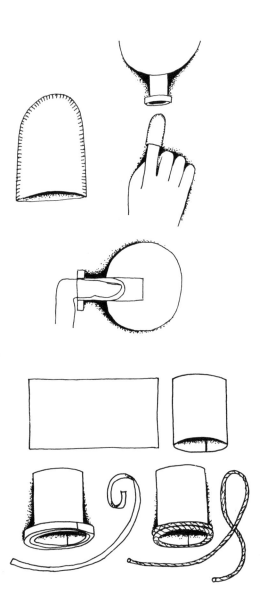

The puppet's neck

The thickness of the neck tube depends on the number of fingers used for controlling the puppet's head. You can use one, two or three fingers. If you control the head with two fingers, use toilet paper rolls. If you have no tube that fits your fingers, make one by rolling a piece of cardboard and gluing it together.

The tube can reach far into the head, but outside the head it should reach only to the second joint on your finger. You move the head by bending the finger joint. Glue a small cloth bag inside the tube to stop your finger at the right place. This makes the head fit firmly on the finger and comfortable to wear. Instead of a bag, you can stuff the tube with kapok and line it with foam rubber.

So that the puppet's costume does not fall off, make a rim by gluing a strip of cardboard or a cord round the bottom of the neck. Use a lot of glue to make the rim very strong.

The top picture shows the royal family for *The Tinder Box* (page 132). Instructions begin on page 34. The puppets in the bottom picture are made from the same pattern, on pages 44–45. The pattern for the waistcoat is on page 42.

Vegetable puppets

Colourful puppets can be made from vegetables. They can be used for only one performance, but they are quick and easy to make — and they can be eaten afterwards! Decorate the puppets with parsley hair, raisin eyes, lettuce-leaf wings and other things, which can be pinned on. Put a garden stick into the head. Slip a piece of material with a hole in the centre on the stick, and tie at the head. You work the puppet by moving the stick.

Birds, fish and other animals need no costumes, but so that the audience does not see the sticks, paint them black and give your theatre a dark backcloth.

Potato heads

Potatoes with funny shapes are very suitable for puppet heads. Wash the potatoes and then cut the features. Broken-off matches can be pushed into the mouth as teeth. Glue on a cottonwool nose, hair and beard, or paint eyes, nose and mouth with a felt-tip pen. The potato head puppet on page 109 was painted yellowish-green with a felt-tip pen.

Living oranges

Cut out eyes, nose and mouth on some oranges. Place a piece of material over a drinking glass and put the orange heads on top, as in the bottom drawing. By pulling the material carefully you can make the heads move up, down, and sideways.

Stands for making heads

When you are making puppet heads, a good stand is a great help. Make a stand by nailing a piece of broom handle to a piece of wood, use a funnel turned upside down, or fill a bottle with sand and push a stick into it for the head to rest on. If the neck opening is wider than the stick, glue paper around the stick.

Heads from tubular gauze

Tubular gauze can be bought at chemists'. This circular-knitted cotton is very elastic and good for reinforcing a head and giving it texture.

Make the basic shape of the head (see page 17). Apply glue to the whole head and pull a piece of tubular gauze over it. The gauze will go into all corners without creasing. Gather the gauze at the back of the neck or on top of the head so that it will be covered by the puppet's hair. Paint the head when the glue is dry. The girl puppet at the bottom of page 13 is made in this way.

Gauze heads made over Plasticine

Plasticine is very good for shaping heads. You can use the same lump of it again and again, and make as many differnt heads as you wish.

Shape a head from Plasticine and fix it to a stand. Cover the head with small, moistened pieces of tissue paper. They must go into all corners and follow the shape very accurately.

Then paste 4 or 5 layers of pieces of gauze on the tissue paper. When the gauze is dry, in a few days, cut the head in two and remove the Plasticine. Then fix the head pieces together again with another layer of gauze. Make a rim at the bottom of the neck.

When the last gauze layer is dry, smooth the head with sandpaper and level off any uneven places with Polyfilla. When this is dry, sand it again. When it is smooth, paint the head.

Eyes
Painted eyes may seem a little dull on a puppet. You can make lively eyes using buttons, glass beads, sequins, or drawing pins. Try which is most effective for the various puppets.

Hair and beard
There is no end of possibilities for giving the puppets hair and beards to suit them. You can use wool, raffia, thread, cottonwool, string, or strips of paper, foil or fabric.

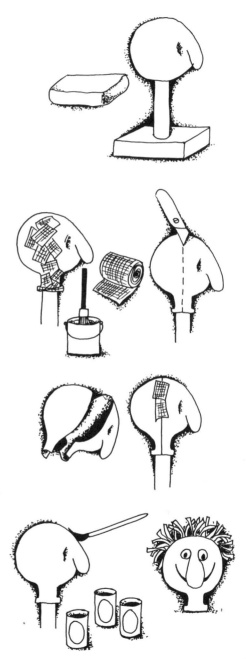

23

Hands

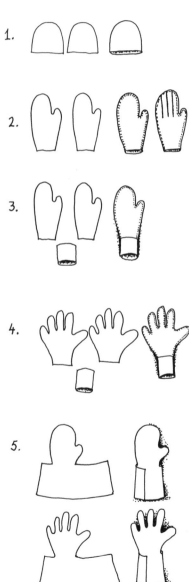

1.

2.

3.

4.

5.

Since puppets, in contrast to real actors, have so few effects to use, we must make the most of what they do have. The hands are one of the puppet's effects. You can make puppets without hands, but it is much more effective if a puppet waves or claps its hands instead of just fluttering its sleeves.

The form and material of the hands should match the rest of the body. A divine princess must have small, delicate hands, whereas a big simpleton must have large, coarse paws. If a puppet has a fabric head, give it fabric hands; if it has a papier mâché head, give it papier mâché hands, etc. Felt hands go well with most materials, and felt is strong and easy to work with.

Various ways of making hands
1 The simplest hands are made by sewing material to the sleeves. This has been done with the puppets on page 19.
2 A felt mitten is an easy and effective hand. Cut out two pieces for each hand, following the pattern on page 25. Do not allow for seams. Oversew pieces together from the right side, and perhaps sew three lines for fingers. Now sew the hands to the costume sleeves.

3 Make felt hands as above, but fill them with kapok and glue them round cardboard tubes into which you can push your finger. Glue the tubes to the costume. This makes the puppet's arms longer because your fingers will not reach right into the hands.

4 The puppet need not have mitten hands; at the bottom right is a pattern for a hand with four fingers, which is easier than one with five fingers and looks just as correct on a puppet.

5 You can make hands from cardboard too. The wide piece at the wrist is folded and glued to fit round your finger.

Large hands

Make the hands very large in relation to the head and body. This looks amusing, and the puppet can express himself even better with his hands movements.

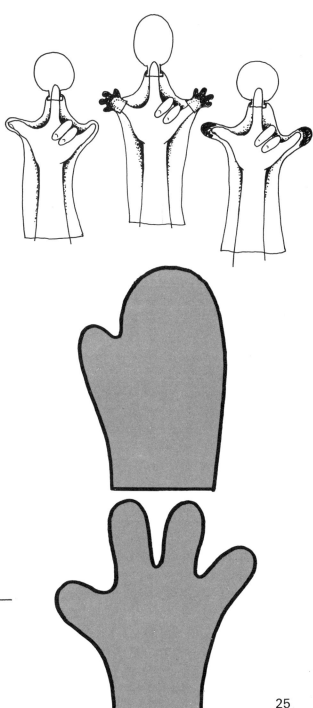

25

A gauze ghost

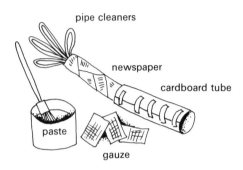

pipe cleaners

newspaper

cardboard tube

paste

gauze

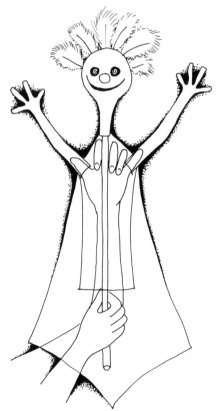

Here is how to make a horrifying, haunting ghost. Make a head from gauze over Plasticine as described on page 22. Paint it white, with black eye sockets and mouth. Glue on two small trinkets or glass beads as eyes.

Bend pipe cleaners for fingers and push them into rolled-up newspaper. Push the rolled-up newspaper into a cardboard tube that fits your finger. Paste small pieces of gauze all over the arms, then paint them white.

The ghost has an underglove and a covering costume. The underglove is made from white cotton fabric. Follow the pattern and instructions on page 32.

The outer costume is made of a square piece of sheer fabric — about 90 cm × 90 cm (3′ × 3′). Cut a hole in the centre and sew it to the neck opening of the underglove. Cut two holes for the ghost's arms and sew them to the arm-holes on the underglove. Glue the head to the neck opening and arms to arm-holes.

The hair can be made from white feathers or cottonwool. The drawing on the left shows how the puppet is worked by both hands, with a stick or broom handle glued into the head.

Glove puppets

The puppets in the drawings are called glove puppets because you put them on your hand like a glove. They can be made to look incredibly alive if you learn to move them correctly and link their movements with voice and sound. They can bow, nod, shake their heads, grasp things, embrace each other and much more. Pages 48 to 51 tell you how to bring your glove puppets to life.

Finger positions
Before making a puppet, decide how you prefer to use your fingers. The width of the neck opening and the style of the costume depend on this. The drawings show the various ways you can hold glove puppets. Drawings B and F show the method used most. Here the distance from the centre of the puppet to the hands is about equal and the shoulders do not slant so much. But whether the shoulders slant is less important than finding the finger position that suits you best. Try the different possibilities.

Drawing G is a mixture of a glove and a rod puppet. The head is placed on a small rod held between the fingers. By rolling the rod to and fro, the puppet can turn its head.

The costume

When you have found the most comfortable finger position, make the costume. Its size depends on the size of your hand. Patterns, diagrams, and instructions for various costumes are on pages 30–32. You can make a simple costume without sleeves, or an elaborate costume and an underglove.

Important points about costumes

Always make the costume long enough to cover your arm from view. It is best for the costume to reach down to your elbow.

Make the sleeves only long enough for your fingers to reach out to the ends. Then the puppet can grasp things.

Make the glove roomy enough for your hand. If it is too baggy, you can always make a few folds in it.

If you are going to use the puppet a lot, make the costume from strong material; if possible, make an underglove and an outer costume.

Costume material

The costume's style and material help to create the puppet's personality, so it is important to choose material and colours to suit the puppet's head and its part in the performance. A princess is not really elegant dressed in a dark costume of coarse material, and a tramp does not look shabby in a silk costume. Try to find some fabric that suits the figure. You can also make the costume completely neutral, for example,

wrong   right

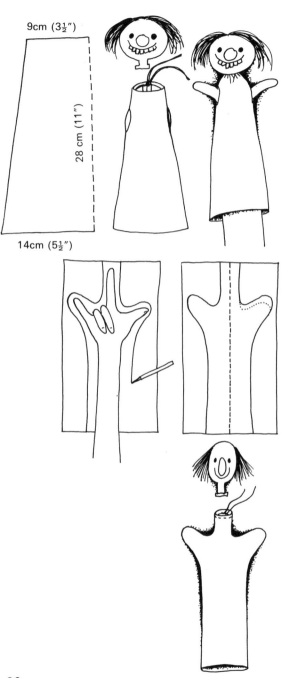

9cm (3½")

28 cm (11")

14cm (5½")

black. Then the puppet's head and hands become the most important parts. You can emphasize the hands by enlarging them as described on page 25.

Costume without sleeves

The easiest costume to make is with the fingers sticking out through two holes as the puppet's arms. On the left is a pattern with measurements. The hand measurements are those of a girl of ten, so they may not fit your hand. First make a pattern from old material to see whether it should be larger or smaller. Adjust the pattern and cut out the costume. Sew the material together at the back of the puppet. Fold down the edge at the top, make a channel, and pull a piece of string or elastic through it. Tie the costume round the puppet's neck — remember to make a rim at the bottom of the neck. Cut two holes for your fingers in the sides of the costume. Hem the costume at the bottom. See the three puppets on page 9.

Costumes with sleeves

Start by making a pattern. Lay your hand on a piece of paper, positioning the fingers as if you had a puppet on your hand. Draw an outline of your hand a little outside the fingers and arm. The puppet's arms will not be straight or of the same length, nor need they be. To make a costume that is the same on both sides, fold the paper along the centre line and cut it out following the larger half. Now make a trial glove: cut out two pattern pieces from old material. Sew them together, leaving openings at the top and bottom. Put on the glove; alter the pattern if you want the glove to be larger or smaller. When the pattern is adjusted, make the actual costume. Make a channel at the neck with an elastic band inside; then you can change heads on the costume. A channel with a wire inside it at the bottom of the costume makes it easier to take off and put on quickly. Also make a loop here so that the puppet can hang on a hook when not in use. To give the puppet hands, see page 24.

Underglove and outer costume

To make a really lasting puppet, first make an underglove from strong material. The instructions are on page 32. If the puppet has hands, sew them to the underglove. Then dress the underglove in frocks, trousers, coats, etc. Sew the clothes to the bottom of the underglove so that during a performance your hand does not go in the wrong place by mistake and you cannot get the puppet on your hand properly and quickly enough.

Puppet with several heads

If you make a neutral costume with a little bag at the top, as in the drawing (right), you can change the heads quickly, using the same costume for many characters.

A roomy costume

To make a roomy costume with a good fit, make the back of the costume larger than the front. In this way the arms will turn forward as your fingers will when you put on the puppet. The pattern for this costume is at the top of these pages. Alter it to fit your hand, or make your own pattern as follows:

Draw an outline of your hand in the finger position you prefer. It may look like drawing A or B. Make the front piece a little narrower and the back piece a little wider, and make a dart at the back of the neck. Lay the pattern on on the material and cut it out, allowing a little extra for the hem. Sew the dart first, and then sew the front and back pieces together. Make a channel for elastic at the top and hem the bottom edge.

centre back fold

centre front fold

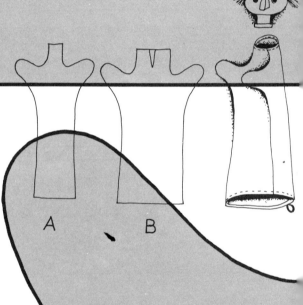

A

B

centre front and back fold

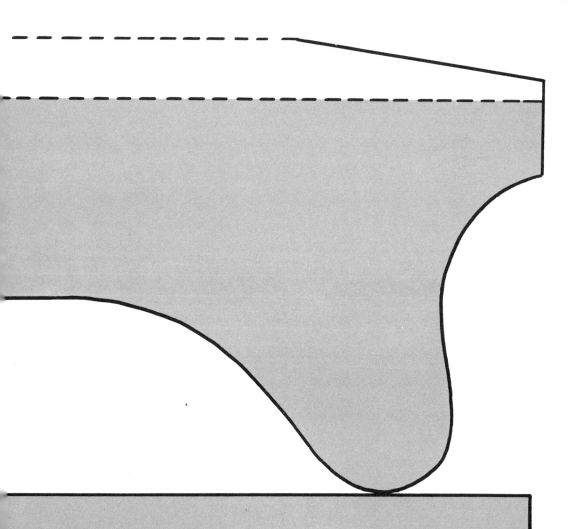

One-piece puppet

This bottom pattern is for a puppet whose head and body are in one piece. It is meant to have the three middle fingers in the head and the little finger and thumb each in a sleeve. Cut out two pieces according to the pattern and sew them together. Decorate it with wool, ribbons, buttons, etc. Eyes, nose and mouth can be sewn or glued on.

Puppets for *The Tinder Box*

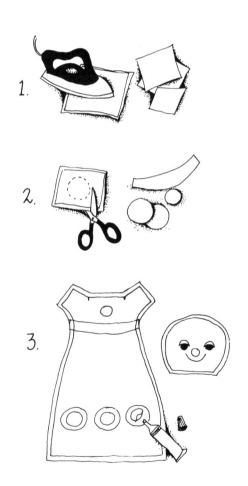

1.

2.

3.

These are puppets for Hans Christian Andersen's fairytale *The Tinder Box*. The story is on page 132. The puppets can also be used for other plays, and you can use different puppets for *The Tinder Box*.

The puppets are a royal family, a soldier, a witch, a dog and a movable tree. The royal family puppets, pictured on page 19, are made entirely from material and are worked by inserting three fingers in the head and the little finger and thumb into the arms.

The royal family

You will need: plain cotton fabric — fancy fabric remnants for costumes — iron-on Vilene — white wool — bits of black and white felt — colourless adhesive.

The patterns are on pages 44–45. Use the same pattern for all the costumes except the king's; his is a little narrower, which is shown by a broken line on the pattern. The puppet heads differ a little, but the heads of the queen and the lady-in-waiting are the same.

For each puppet cut out two pieces of plain cotton fabric for the head and four pieces for the hands, and one front and one back costume piece from fancy fabric remnants. The back piece is wider than the front to give the hand ample room. Allow about 1 cm ($\frac{3}{8}$") for seams

Draw the features on the fabric and oversew along all hems. Now follow the drawings:

1 Iron-on Vilene is treated on one side (the shiny side) with glue that fuses with the fabric when ironed on. Iron Vilene to the back of the fabric being used to decorate the costume and face: the shiny side of the Vilene must face the fabric and the iron must be hot.

2 Cut out the pieces; the Vilene prevents them from fraying. Cut eyes and eyelids from felt.

3 Glue the pieces to faces and costumes. If the material is thin, apply only a thin layer of glue. When glue is dry, stitch round the decorations. Beads can be sewn on too.

4 Sew hands to the front and back costume pieces. Sew the costume together, wrong side out, leaving an opening between the Xs in the drawing. Cut small notches in the seams under the arms. Turn the costume right side out.

Sew head parts together, wrong side out, leaving the neck edge open. Turn right side out, and on the king's head sew through both layers along the dotted line on the pattern. Stuff a little kapok in the heads, but leave enough room for your fingers.

5 Sew a draw thread at neck on back of costume and pull it to the same width as front neck. Sew on the head; remember not to sew through all the layers at once, as your fingers must reach into the head. For hair, sew wool down centre of head, back-stitching from forehead to neck.

Make a crown from a strip of fabric with Vilene on the back. Glue on some ornaments, decorate with stitching, and sew the crown together to form a ring. For the princess, sew a cape to the crown.

Other puppets from the same pattern
The royal family patterns can be used for many other figures. You can see some suggestions at the bottom of page 19.

The soldier

You will need: plain cotton fabric – blue, white, red and brown felt – turquoise fabric – brown wool – kapok – buttons – adhesive – snap fasteners – cardboard.

The soldier is made of an underglove reaching his waist and a covering costume — the jacket — to which two legs are sewn. Your hand goes in the glove under the jacket. The glove, which has elastic at the bottom, fits firmly round the wrist. Wear a long black glove to hide your arm from the audience.

The patterns for the soldier are on pages 43–44. Allow 1 cm ($\frac{3}{8}$″) for seams. Cut head and body from plain cotton fabric, jacket from blue felt, and boots from brown felt. For legs, cut two pieces of turquoise fabric 8 cm × 14 cm

($3\frac{1}{4}$″ × $5\frac{1}{2}$″), and sew them to make two tubes. Sew eyes and nose on the face. Sew head pieces together, wrong side out, leaving the neck edge open. Turn right side out and sew through both layers along the dotted line on the pattern. Stuff kapok in head, leaving enough room for your fingers. Sew the body together, wrong side out, and turn it right side out. Sew a draw thread at neck on back piece and pull it to the same width as the front neck. Sew head and body together. Sew a channel with elastic in it at bottom of body. Using backstitch, sew on bunches of wool for hair.

Sew the jacket together, wrong side out, leaving the neck edge open. Turn right side out, fold over and glue down the edges. Sew on shiny buttons, and glue on red and white felt straps, as in the picture. Make the belt loose and slip a cardboard sword through it. Cut the jacket back up the middle and sew on snap fasteners. In this way the puppet can change costumes. Sew on legs under front edge of jacket. Fold over and glue down bottom edges of legs. Sew 3 pieces of boot together. Stuff boots, sew on 'laces', push up into legs and sew on.

The witch

You will need: green, violet and orange fabric – violet, purple, black and white felt – green wool – kapok – adhesive.

Cut body from violet fabric using pattern for king on pages 44–45; allow for seams. Sew together wrong side out and turn. Sew draw thread at neck on back and pull to same width as front neck.

Cut the head in green material, using the pattern on page 42. Cut back of head in two along dotted line on pattern. Cut eyes, mouth and teeth from felt, glue them on and stitch round them. Sew the two back head pieces to the front, wrong side out. There will be an opening across the back of the neck for your fingers. Sew the bottom edge of this opening to the front of the body, and the top edge to the back. The witch's chin will hang down on the chest. Fill head with kapok, leaving enough room for your fingers. Cut 2 nose pieces in orange material, using the pattern on page 42. Sew together on wrong side, leaving straight edge open. Turn right side out, fill with kapok, and sew to face.

Sew green wool on the head for hair and make a hat from violet felt. Read about making hats on page 57. Crotchet a shawl for the witch from violet wool, or find a suitable piece of material.

The dog with big eyes

The dog with the big eyes can be made from teddy-bear material. It can move its mouth and is made the same way as the dog on page 66. The two body sections, for which there are no patterns, are each 30 cm (12") long, 11 cm (4½") at the top, and 24 cm (9½") at the bottom. Patterns for head and legs are on pages 40–41.

The living tree

The hollow tree the soldier climbs down to fetch the tinder box can move its branches, and open and close. It is two gloves sewn together, your fingers being the branches. Make the pattern by drawing the outline of your fingers on a piece of folded paper. Place the little finger right up against the fold and draw a little away from the fingers. Cut out the pattern and unfold the paper. Cut two pieces of towelling in this pattern. Sew the parts together from the right side. Stitch down the centre (dotted line in drawing) through both layers so that the glove is divided in two. Sew front edges of gloves to a tube of fabric fitting round your arms. Make the tube rather wide at the bottom, as it is hard to keep your elbows together. Do not sew the rear edge of the gloves to the tube. By leaving an opening here you can, for example, make a bird on a long stick come up through the tube and peep over the treetop. You can also make things disappear into the tree trunk.

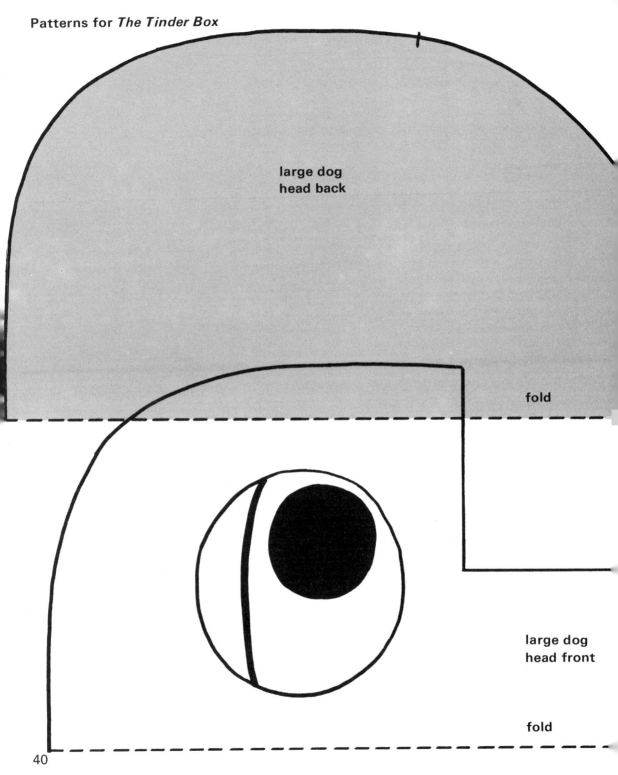

Patterns for *The Tinder Box*

large dog
head back

fold

large dog
head front

fold

40

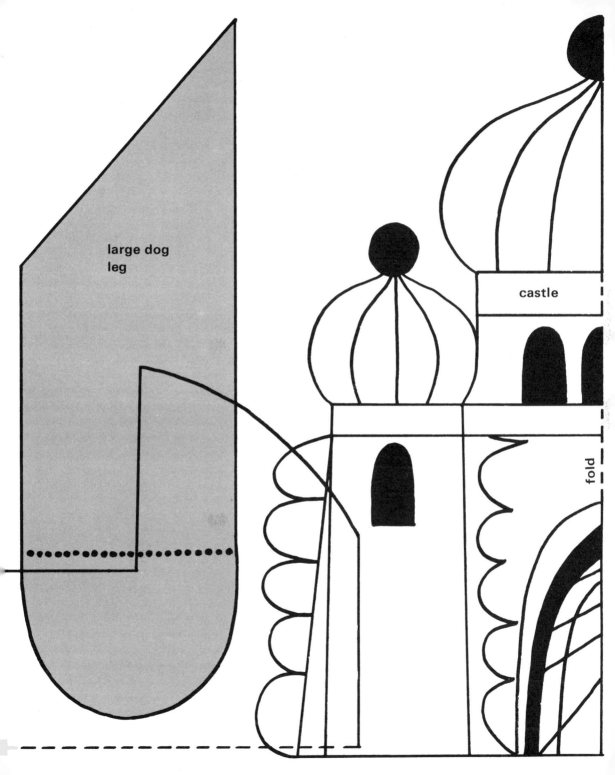

large dog
leg

castle

fold

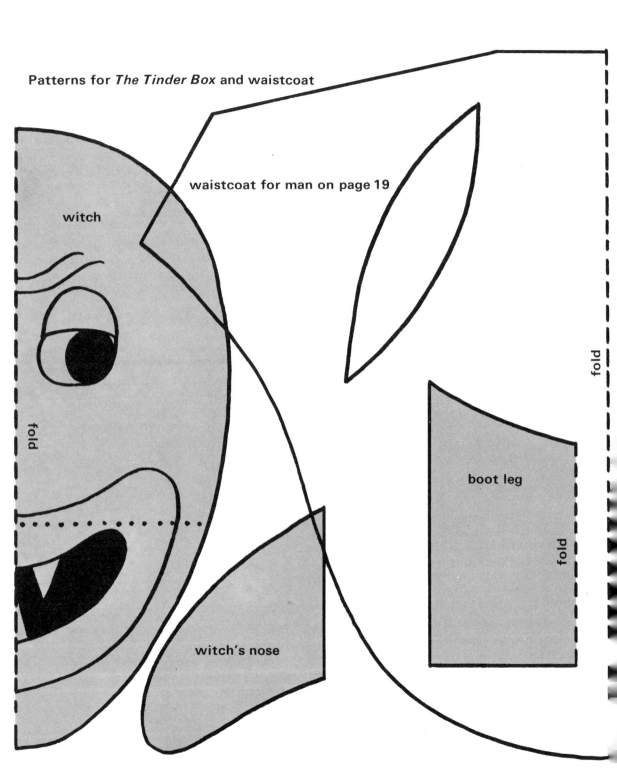

Patterns for *The Tinder Box* and waistcoat

witch

waistcoat for man on page 19

fold

fold

boot leg

fold

witch's nose

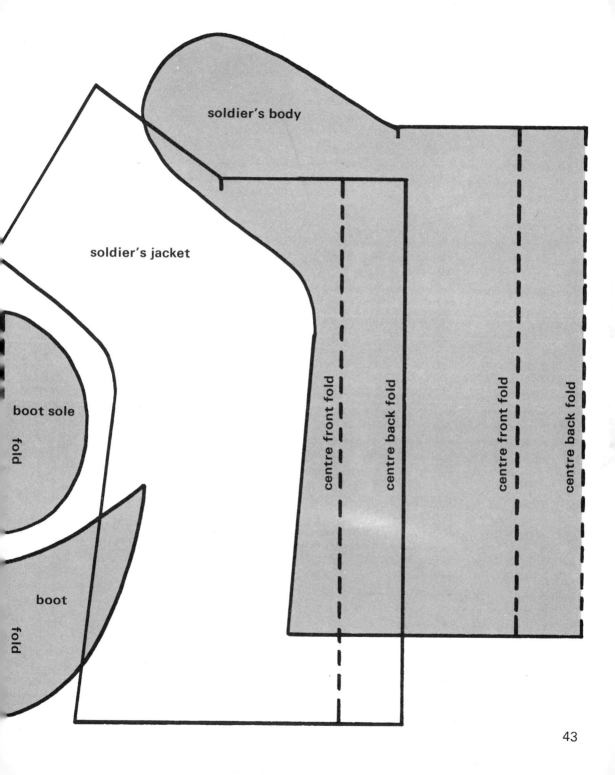

soldier's body

soldier's jacket

boot sole

fold

boot

fold

centre front fold

centre back fold

centre front fold

centre back fold

43

Patterns for *The Tinder Box*

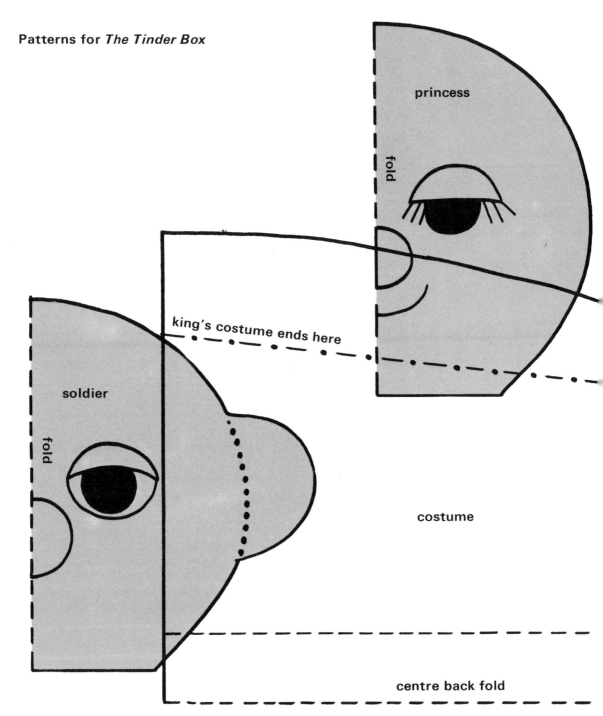

princess

fold

king's costume ends here

soldier

fold

costume

centre back fold

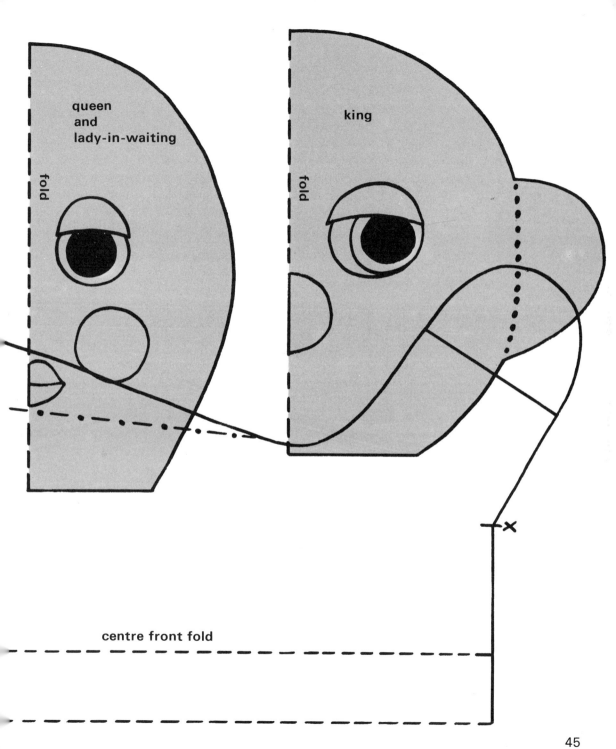

queen
and
lady-in-waiting

fold

king

fold

centre front fold

x

45

Glove puppets with legs

To give glove puppets legs, sew two tubes of fabric to the front of the costume. The best way is to hide the sewing under a jacket or a dress. Do not make the legs from stiff fabric or stuff them too firmly; let them hang down loosely and flap about.

You can make shoes or boots from felt or papier mâché, or from foam rubber with fabric glued on.

You can make your performance more life-like if the puppets have legs. For example, try sitting the puppet on the edge of the stage with its legs dangling in front of it. Then let it take one leg in its hands (that is, your fingers) and cross it over the other. Or make the puppet move across the stage as shown in the drawing at the bottom of the next page.

Let the puppet sit on the stage with bent legs, sideways to the audience, while you hold its heels with your free hand — without the audience seeing your fingers. Stretch out its legs with your free hand. Let it sit still for a moment. Then push the body forward so that its legs are bent again. In this way it can move to and fro, and even climb a tree.

You can also make the puppet stamp on the floor by moving its leg with your free hand. The sound can be made louder if you stamp on the floor in time with the puppet's movements.

Giving the
puppet life

The finished puppet is, in fact, only a casing of material with a face that keeps the same expression all the time. Even if your puppet is very smart or funny to look at, the performance still depends on you making the puppet come alive in front of the audience — and you do this with your voice and hand movements.

It is important that the puppet's appearance, movements and voice suit its part in the play. An old man usually moves slowly in a stooped position and speaks slowly too. A smart young fellow has lively movements and a light voice.

Use a mirror
To find the right position and movements for the puppet, practise in front of a mirror. You can then see what is most effective, and you are better able to make voice and movements suit each other.

The voice
When you are acting a play, it is very important to speak clearly and distinctly so that everyone can hear what you are saying. And it is very important that you make your voice suit the

puppet's part. If the puppet is afraid and you cry "Help!" in an ordinary voice, the audience will not believe that the puppet is afraid. You must scream "HELP!" with horror and fear in your voice. If the puppet is playing an elegant lady, try to give it the voice and movements of an elegant lady; and if your puppet is a nasty fellow, then speak as creepily as you can.

Working the puppet

You will find that it is hard work to work a glove puppet correctly. As a beginner you will probably hold the puppets in a lop-sided way, and lower them further and further behind the stage as the performance goes on. In the end the audience can only see the tops of their heads. It is simply because your arm gets tired.

You can avoid this with an elbow-board like the one on page 115. You can sit down during the performance, but there is more opportunity for moving the puppet if you stand up and hold it with your arm stretched above your head. It is also easier to make the puppet's walk and turns look right if you walk along the floor and turn round when the puppet does. Of course your arms will get tired, but with practice and when you are carried away with the performance, you will often not feel it until the performance is over.

Keep the puppet straight

Keep the puppet straight as much as you can whether it walks, stands, nods or spreads out its arms. It looks wrong if the puppet leans to one side, or curves forwards or backwards.

right   right   wrong

wrong   right

The hips

Although the puppet should be held straight, it can bow, lean forwards and backwards, and turn from side to side. But the movements must be from the puppet's hips — that means your wrist. With practice you will be able to make many good movements.

To make a solemn bow hold the puppet vertically with its arms together in front. Move it a little towards the audience. Now bend your wrist, and at the same time spread its arms and draw your elbow back a little. Then let the puppet return to an upright position.

The head

Whether the puppet cries or smiles, its face will look the same. Therefore you must express its emotions in other ways.

The puppet can nod and shake its head; bend its head down between its arms and weep; bend its head backward in surprise, spreading out its arms at the same time; or look thoughtful by bending its head to one side and resting it on one arm.

The arms

You can create the most expressive movements with the puppet's arms — your fingers. But take care not to exaggerate the arm movements. If the puppet sticks out its arms all the time and moves them to and fro with every word, the effect on the audience will be somewhat confusing. Find a basic position for the puppet to hold its arms in, for example, folded on the tummy. Then only move its arms when there is reason for it.

It can move one arm or both to emphasize certain words. It can point, clap or rub its hands together. Two puppets can fight or embrace lovingly. When puppets are fighting, it is very funny if you emphasize the blows by smacking yourself on the thigh or banging on a bucket turned upside down. You can read more about using sounds on page 124. If you want to make a puppet moan and cry, bend its head forward, put its arms up over its ears, and rock its body to and fro.

Puppets can grasp things, and this is something you can make a lot of in your performance. They can carry things around, hand them to each other, and place them on the stage.

Here is a play in which several different arm movements can be used: A thief steals something. A policeman catches the thief and beats him with a truncheon. The unconscious scoundrel hangs limply over the edge of the stage. You carefully withdraw your hand from the thief's costume; the policeman then grasps him under his arm and carries him off.

Puppet with a big tummy

To make a funny puppet with a large tummy, stuff a round bag and sew it inside the costume. Then push your hand up behind the bag. You can also make a tummy from papier mâché over a balloon (see page 90).

Elegant lady with a hat

To make this elegant lady use the pattern for the head on page 104 and for the hand on page 25.

Cut 4 pieces for the head and 2 pieces for each hand from felt; do not allow for seams. Oversew the head pieces together from the right side, with small stitches. Stuff the head with kapok. For the eyes, work a strong thread right through the head and make a little stitch; pull it firmly to form a socket. Then sew on beads or round buttons. Draw a mouth with a black felt-tip pen, and redden the cheeks and nose. Glue a cardboard tube that fits round your finger into the neck.

Oversew the hands together from the right side, using small stitches. Stuff only the extreme end of the fingers, so that there is room for your own.

Make the costume from any fabric, using the top pattern on page 32, allowing 0·6 cm ($\frac{1}{4}$") for seams. Sew the pieces together, wrong side out, leaving neck, hand, and bottom edges open. Turn right side out. Fold over the neck edge and sew on the head. Fold over the rounded edges of the hands, insert felt hands, and sew on. Hem the costume at the bottom. Page 58 tells you how to make the hat.

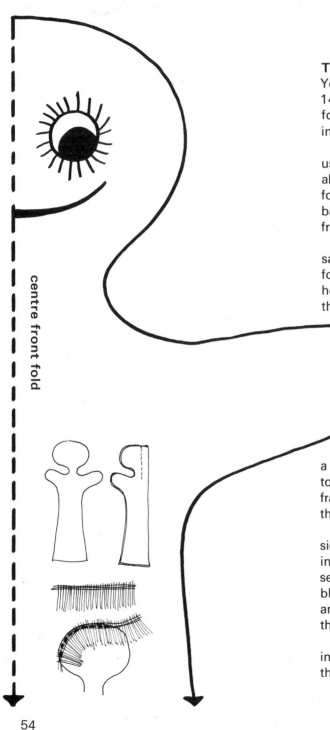

centre front fold

The Fire Man

You can read the story of the Fire Man on page 143. Alfred and Mary are made like the puppets for *The Tinder Box* (see pages 34–45 for instructions).

Cut out the Fire Man from orange material, using the pattern on this page, but making it about 10 cm (4") longer. Use the same pattern for the back, but add 2 cm (1") at the fold. The back, therefore, is 4 cm (2") wider than the front. This makes the puppet fit better.

The front and back of the head must be the same size. Therefore, with the back piece still folded in half, sew through both layers of the head 2 cm (1") from the centre, as shown by the dotted line in the small drawing.

For hair, fray a piece of material so that only a few horizontal threads are holding frays together. Place it against right side of head, frays turning in towards the centre, and sew to the edge.

Sew front and back together with right sides facing. Hem the bottom and cut notches in seams under arms and at neck. Oversew seams and turn right side out. Cut eyes from black and white felt and glue on. Sew eyelashes and mouth with black embroidery cotton. Stuff the head, leaving enough room for your fingers.

The puppet is worked by pushing your index and middle fingers into the head, and thumb and little finger into each of the arms.

Hats

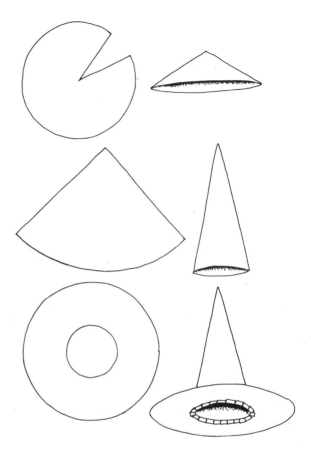

Here are some ideas for hats for your puppets. You can make many different hats from the basic shapes shown on these pages.

Top hats

Make top hats from cardboard covered with glued-on material. Cut a large circle for the brim. Cut a hole in the centre to fit the puppet's head; if you want a tiny hat to sit right on top of the puppet's head, make the hole smaller than the head. Cut a strip the same length as the circumference of the hole (measure with a piece of string), allowing 1 cm ($\frac{1}{2}$") extra for glued area. Cut notches on long edges, and glue strip together to form a tube. At top edge fold notches inwards and glue on the circle cut out of the brim. Push tube into brim, turn bottom notches outwards, and glue in place under brim.

Witch's and clown's hats

These pointed hats can be made from a whole, half or quarter circle, according to how pointed you want them to be. Make them from cardboard or felt, or cardboard covered with glued-on material.

For a clown's hat, bend a circular piece into a cone and glue or sew it together. To make the witch's hat from cardboard, cut notches at the bottom of the cone. Cut a brim to fit circumference of cone, and slip it over cone. Glue notches under brim. If you make the witch's hat from felt, do not cut notches, but sew the cone and brim together.

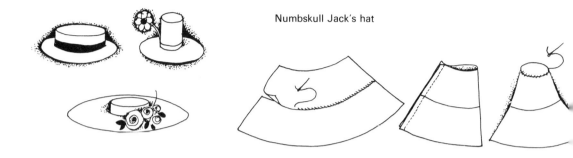

Numbskull Jack's hat

Pirate's hat

To make the fierce pirate's hat on page 56, use pattern C on page 60. If necessary, alter it to fit your puppet's head. Cut out two pieces of cardboard, paint them black and join them along the edge with black adhesive tape. Paint on skull and crossbones, or cut out from white paper and glue on.

Fancy summer hat

The fine summer hat in the picture is made from strong white Vilene. Use pattern A on page 60. The pattern shows only a quarter of a brim; to make pattern for a whole brim, fold paper in half once each way. Place folds on fold lines on pattern, and trace quarter brim. Cut out and unfold the paper and use pattern to cut whole brim. Cut four crown pieces from pattern, allowing 0·6 cm ($\frac{1}{4}$") for seams. Sew crown parts together, and sew crown to brim. Decorate hat with flowers, feathers, a veil, or whatever you please.

Motorcyclist's helmet

The motorcyclist's helmet on page 56 is made from papier mâché over a blown-up balloon. Blow up a balloon until it is a bit bigger than the puppet's head. Paste strips of newspaper all over it. Use many layers to make it strong. When it is dry, pierce the balloon and pull it out. Cut helmet to shape and paste strips along bottom edge to make it neat.

When helmet is dry again, smooth it with sandpaper and paint it.

Numbskull Jack's hat

Numbskull Jack's hat (see page 91) is made of felt. Use pattern B on page 60. The hatched parts on the pattern are seam allowances. Place crown over brim so that it just covers top seam space. Sew together on right side with small hemstitches. Fold hat together wrong side out and stitch back seam. Turn right side out and oversew little circle to top with small stitches. Decorate with a feather.

Patterns for hats

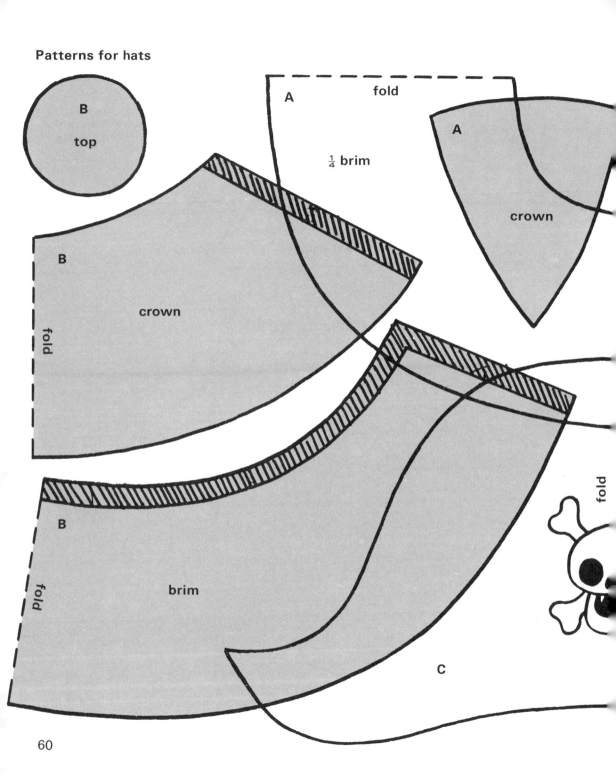

B
top

A

fold

¼ brim

A

crown

B
crown

fold

B
brim

fold

fold

C

The puppets on the cover

The puppets on the book's cover are made from corduroy and decorated with felt. Use the patterns on this page. Cut out the pieces. Glue felt pieces to body fronts. Stitch round decorations, except puppet's beard — sew this only along lower mouth edge. Place body pieces together wrong side out, push wool or felt "hair" between them and sew together. Cut notches in seams under arms, oversew seams and turn. Insert three middle fingers in head and thumb and little finger in arms.

body fold

Animal puppets

Animal heads can be made in the same way as the puppets' heads on pages 16–17; you just give them different features. Animal bodies can be made from the patterns on pages 32–33, but make the hands look like paws. You can also make other shapes for animal puppets. Here are some ideas.

Animal with a large mouth
To work a puppet that can move its mouth, put your thumb in the lower part of the mouth, and the four other fingers in the top part.

To make the mouth rigid, cut two pieces of cardboard (as in drawing A) the same size the mouth is to be; join them with adhesive tape. You can glue straps to the cardboard to keep your fingers in place, but this is not necessary if the animal is sewn together to fit fairly tightly round the cardboard. For the animal, cut two long pieces of material a little larger at the top than the cardboard pieces and large enough for your arm to go in when they are sewn together. Also cut an inner mouth from material. These pieces are shown in drawing B. Sew inner mouth and glove together, wrong side out, sewing first along the two jaws, then down the long seams of the glove (C). Turn right side out and push in pieces of cardboard. Put some kapok on top of the cardboard pieces, leaving enough room for

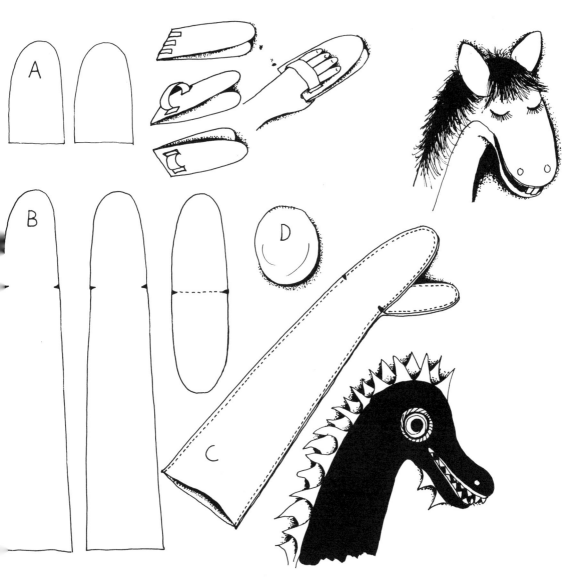

your fingers. To give the animal a high forehead sew a little stuffed bag (D) inside the head. You can also leave the bag free and put it in position — just above the knuckles — when you put the animal on your hand.

Finally, sew on eyes and mane or other decorations. For example, you can make a dragon's mane from felt, teeth from felt or foam rubber, or a nose from a ball of kapok covered in material.

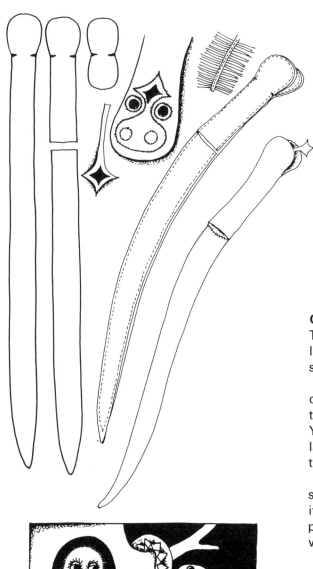

Giant snake

The snake in the picture is two metres (yards) long. It can move its mouth, which is made the same way as the one on the previous page.

The top layer of the body is one long piece of material, but the bottom layer is divided in two. Only the lower end of the snake is stuffed. Your arm goes in the opening in the bottom layer, so you move the snake and fill it out at the same time.

Decorate the top layer with felt, glued or sewn on. Cut the tongue from felt and decorate it. The long mane is made by sewing lots of pieces of wool about 20 cm (8") long on a tape, which you then sew on the snake.

Sew the head pieces together, wrong side out, with the inner mouth between. Then sew the other parts of body together, turn right side out, stuff tail with kapok and sew up the opening in the tail.

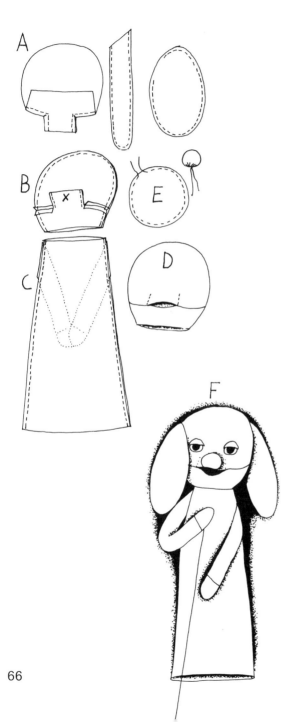

Dog with a movable mouth

Here is how to make the dog shown on page 73. It is not very easy to make and, unless you are very good at sewing, you might want to ask someone to help you.

It can be made from towelling, teddy-bear material, or other thick material.

Cut out the parts from the patterns on pages 68–69, allowing 1 cm ($\frac{3}{8}$") for seams.

A. Fold flap on front of head to right side and sew together as shown by broken line. Cut notches in corners of seams and press seams apart. Sew ears and arms together, and turn right side out.

B. Turn part for inner mouth (x) upwards to wrong side. Sew front and back head sections together, wrong side out, leaving neck open.

C. Stuff kapok into tips of paws. Sew through both layers from right side along dotted line on pattern. Place front and back body pieces together, wrong side out, with paws in between, and sew sides together. Sew head to body and turn right side out.

D. Sew piece for inner mouth to front of head from right side, as shown by broken line. It is sewn on only at sides to make bags for your fingers inside head.

E. Make nose by gathering a piece of material round cottonwool ball. Sew on above mouth.

F. Stuff top part of head, sew on ears and wooden beads for eyes. Hem edge of body.

H

G

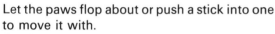

Let the paws flop about or push a stick into one to move it with.

G. You can make many other animals from the same pattern.

H. This drawing shows how you hold the dog and move its mouth.

A little dog

This little dog is for one finger. You can make it from teddy-bear material or something similar.

Cut out two pieces of the pattern on page 70. Remember to allow for seams. Place the parts right side to right side and sew together, except at the bottom. Turn right side out and sew through both layers along dotted lines on the pattern. Cut out four pieces of material 3 cm × 4 cm (1″ × 1½″) for legs and one piece of 3 cm × 8 cm (1″ × 3″) for the tail. Roll them into sausages and hemstitch. Stuff kapok into the head, leaving enough room for your finger. Sew legs and tail to body. Eyes can be made from little pieces of felt sewn on with black glass beads. Glue on a nose made from a cottonwool ball painted black.

Patterns for dog with a movable mouth

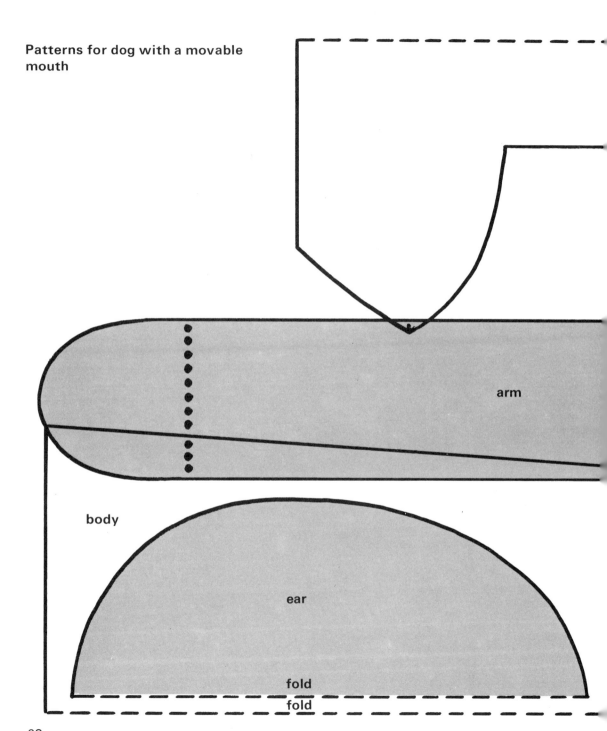

arm

body

ear

fold

fold

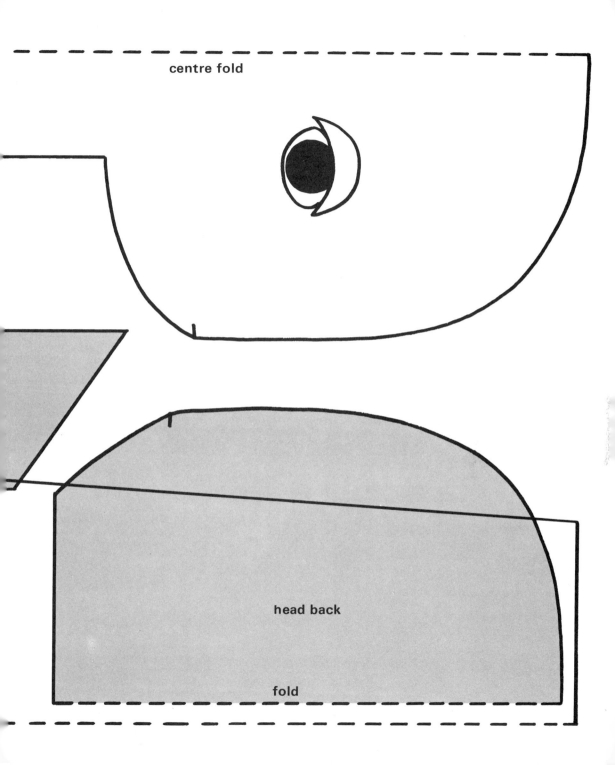

centre fold

head back

fold

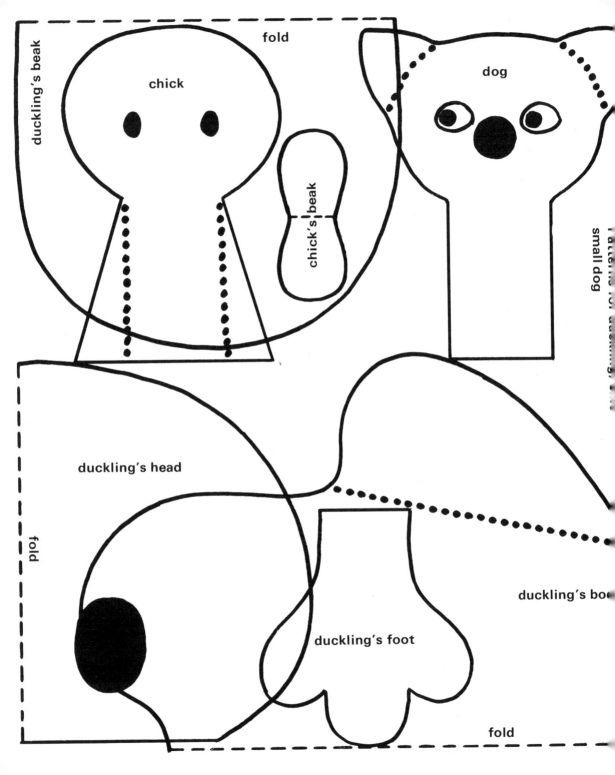

duckling's beak

fold

chick

dog

chick's beak

Patterns for duckling and small dog

duckling's head

fold

duckling's foot

duckling's bo

fold

The Ugly Duckling

The duckling and little chicks on page 73 were made for Hans Christian Andersen's fairytale *The Ugly Duckling*, which is on page 137.

To make the duckling you will need: a piece of ·thick white wool material or felt about 25 cm×60 cm (10"×24") – a piece of brown felt about 16 cm×16 cm (6¼"×6¼") – pink and orange cotton material, each about 14 cm× 24 cm (5½"×9½") – a little black felt – wool remnants – iron-on Vilene – kapok for stuffing.

The patterns are on page 70. Cut pieces for head (2) and body (2) from white material. Cut four feet from brown felt. Cut 1 beak from orange material, two half-beaks from pink material, and two eyes from black felt. Allow 1 cm (⅜") for seams, except on feet and eyes.
1 Place feet together in pairs and oversew from the right side, leaving straight edge open. Stuff with kapok. Place pieces for the body right side to right side with the feet between, so that they are on the inside. Sew together, leaving top edge open.

Glue eyes to one of the head pieces and sew a ring round them. Place front and rear head pieces right side to right side and sew together, leaving bottom edge open. Iron Vilene to the wrong side of beak pieces and place them right side to right side. Sew together along the curved edges, leaving straight edges open.
2 Turn all three pieces right side out. Sew through both layers on body along dotted line on pattern.

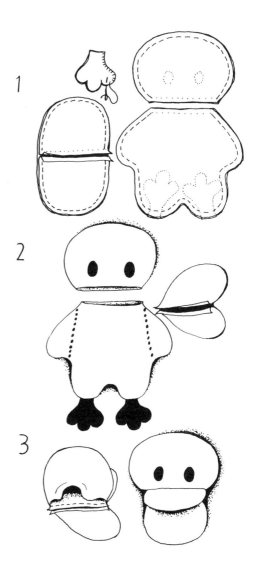

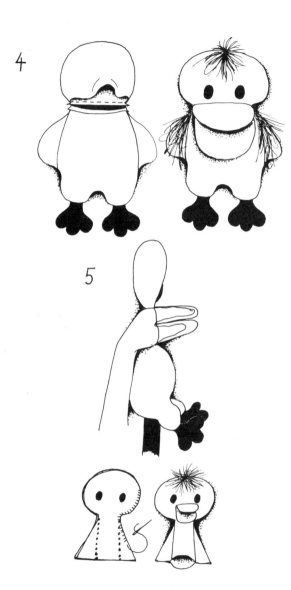

3 Sew front of head to top pink beak.
4 Sew front of body to bottom pink beak.
Stuff head and body. Oversew back of head to
top pink beak, and back of body to bottom
pink beak. Make sure that you can still get
your hand into the beak. Finally, sew wool
remnants to the forehead and wings.
5 This is how to hold the duckling.

Little chicks
The little chicks are held on the fingers. Make
three or four and have a little flock of cheeping
chicks on your hand.

You will need: orange and yellow felt —
yellow wool remnants — black embroidery
yarn — kapok.

Cut two body pieces from yellow felt and a
beak from orange felt, using the patterns on
page 70. There is no seam allowance. Embroider eyes on one body piece and place
pieces together, right side out. Oversew together, leaving bottom edge open. Sew through
both layers along dotted line on the pattern.
Sew bottom edges of wings together. Sew on
beak along fold line and sew or glue bits of
wool to top of head. Put a little kapok into the
head, leaving enough room for your finger.

Directions for making the brown dog are on page 66 and
for the little white dog on page 67.

Owl

The friendly owl in the colour picture can nod its head, turn it from side to side, and flap its wings. It is worked with two hands, the thumbs going into the head and the other fingers into the wings. Head and body are made separately.

You will need: reddish-brown fabric — brown, black and orange felt — two oval glass beads — parcel string — kapok — pipe cleaners — colourless adhesive.

Using patterns on pages 76—77, cut two head pieces and front and rear body pieces from fabric. Cut four wings, beak and feet from brown felt.

The head Sew front and rear of head together from right side, leaving neck open between As on pattern. Stuff with kapok. Make two cardboard tubes to fit round your thumbs and glue them into head (see drawing).

The eyes are made of circles of brown, orange and black felt, and glass beads; eyelids of brown felt and lashes of string. Glue pieces in place and stitch round eyes. Sew beak together, stuff with kapok and sew to head. For hair, sew 10 cm (4") lengths of string in tufts all round head, using backstitch.

The body Glue small orange felt circles to body front and stitch round them. Sew darts together. Sew front and back pieces together, wrong side out, leaving opening between Bs on pattern. Turn right side out and stuff. Oversew feet togehter in pairs from right side. Push pipe cleaners into claws and stuff. Push feet into body at Bs on pattern and sew in place. Sew up opening between legs. Sew string fringe along neck.

The wings Sew wings together in pairs from right side, with lengths of string between pieces at bottom edge, leaving open edges

facing body. Stitch along dotted line on pattern to make pocket for your fingers, and work decorative stitching round it. Glue or sew orange felt scallops to bottom as in picture. Sew front edge of wings to sides of body. Wearing long black gloves, push your thumbs into the head and your other fingers into the wings.

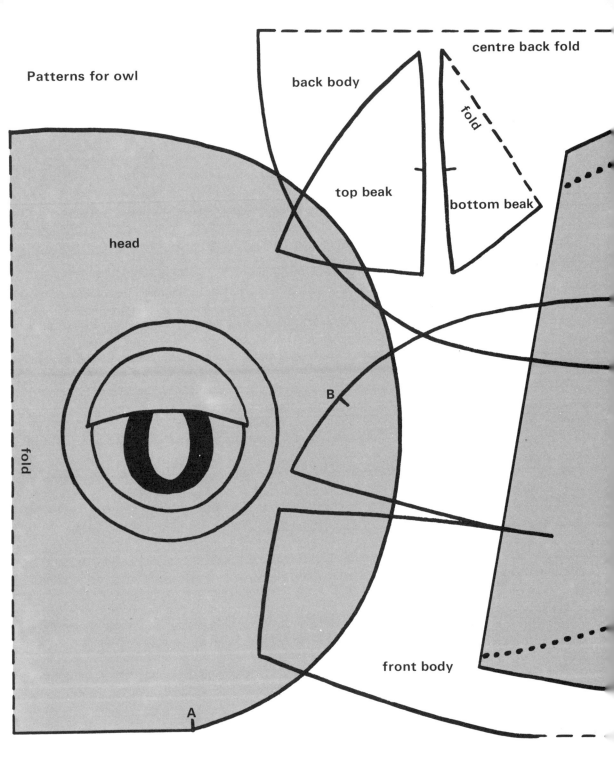

Patterns for owl

head

fold

A

B

back body

top beak

bottom beak

centre back fold

fold

front body

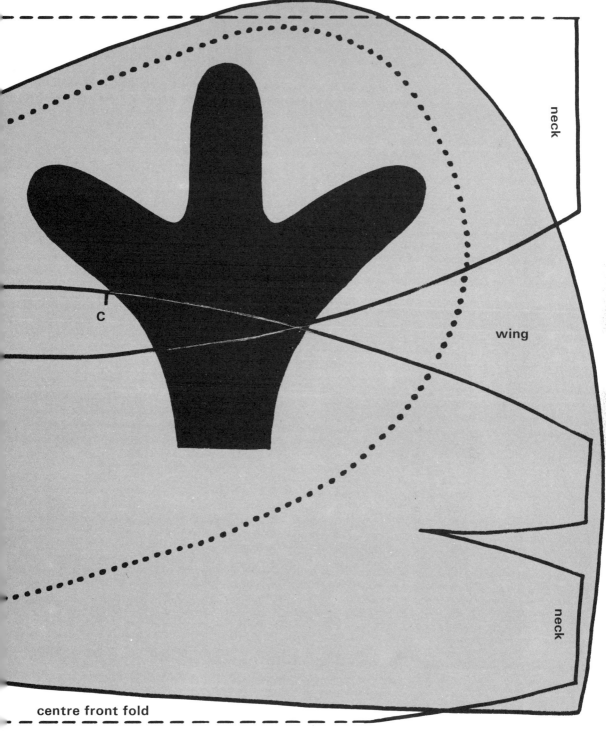

neck

wing

c

neck

centre front fold

77

Rod puppets

You work the rod puppet, as the words suggest, on a rod, or rods, often using both hands. One hand holds a rod with the puppet's head and body while the other works one of the puppet's arms with another rod, as you will see in some of the drawings here. It is rather difficult to work both puppet arms on rods unless there are two of you. A mixture of a glove and a rod puppet can be made by working a puppet's head with one hand and its arms with a rod, like the dog on page 66, or you can work the head on a rod and the arms with your fingers, like the ghost on page 26 and the wooden figures on page 100.

You can use all kinds of materials for making rod puppets: egg trays, cotton reels, boxes, cardboard, plastic bottles and many other things. Here are some ideas.

Broom handle and wooden ball
Get a piece of broom handle 15 cm – 20 cm (6"–8") long and a wooden ball, which you can buy in most handcraft shops. Glue the wooden ball on the broom handle. Smooth the other end of the broom handle with sandpaper.

Paint a face on the wooden ball. If you varnish it afterwards, the head will look really splendid and the colours will be more lasting. Glue on wool for hair. You can also make a felt costume and glue it round the broom handle.

This is how the puppets in the little orange theatre on page 109 are made.

Broom handle costume

Cut a circle from a piece of thin, soft material — perhaps lining material. Cut a small hole in the centre. Put the circle on the puppet and glue it at the neck with a piece of bias binding on top. This smart costume will hide your hand and make the puppet very suitable as a dancing puppet because the material will swing round when it moves.

Arms

At the bottom of the page are some rod puppets that can move their arms in different ways. The first — the fellow with the cold and the big nose — can turn his head because it is on a rod pushed through a cardboard tube. His shoulders are a piece of wood tied to the cardboard tube; his arms are round sticks connected with loops. His hands can be made from wood or foam rubber covered with gauze. Make loops on the hands into which rods are pushed and bent over. The singer in the centre has movable fabric arms. His body is a long and a short rod crossed at shoulder level. The little devil on the right has arms of twisted pipe cleaners that hold up his costume. Head and hands are made of felt.

How to work the arms

The drawing at the top left of this page shows how to hold a puppet's body and head with one rod and work its arm with another. The drawing on the right shows how to hold a puppet and work both its arms by rods.

Suitable rods

For large puppets, glue a piece of broom handle in the head. Otherwise, sticks and garden stakes of different thicknesses are suitable for holding a puppet's body and head, and working its arms. You can also use thick wire for working the arms.

Easy cardboard puppets

Cut simple, funny puppets from stiff drawing paper, cardboard, or cardboard boxes. Paint them and glue them to rods made of card. Cardboard used for boxes consists of two layers with a corrugated piece in between, as in the drawing centre left. If you make puppets from this cardboard, keep the grooves vertical and hold the puppet with a knitting needle or stick pushed into a groove.

Moving cardboard puppets

The bottom drawing shows puppets with movable arms and legs. To make them, cut arms and legs separately from cardboard and fix them to the puppet with a paper fastener the kind used for closing envelopes.

Fix wire or cardboard rods to the arms with a paper fastener in the puppet's hand. The goose's neck has several links and, therefore is very movable.

Giant puppets

Besides playing with little puppets in your theatre, you can make yourself into a giant puppet like one of those you see in these drawings.

The two top puppets have cardboard tube necks that fit your head. Tapes attached to the neck are tied under your chin to keep the big head in place. Make the heads from foam rubber with gauze glued on top or from papier mâché over a balloon. Make the hands from foam rubber or stuff an old mitten with kapok or put your hand in it.

The boy in the bottom left drawing fixed a clothes hanger to a rod and hung an old jacket over it. Then he crawled into the jacket. He is holding the rod with one hand and using the other to control the puppet's hand.

The girl on the right is working a giant rod puppet with a movable hand.

Foam rubber rod puppets

The man and the bird in the pictures are made from foam rubber cut to shape, with pieces of gauze pasted over. The rods the puppets are held with are secured with household glue, after drilling a hole in the puppet.

The rod holding the man's head goes right down through the body. It is not glued in, so the head can be turned and pushed up and down. His arms are made of fabric glued to the shoulders. Sticks have been pushed into his foam rubber hands to work them. The puppet is painted. When working with foam rubber, remember to use only a water-based adhesive.

Rod puppets with living hands

To make an amusing rod puppet, let one of your hands be the puppet's hand, while you hold the rod with the puppet's head with the other. This kind of puppet is very easy to work and can do many funny things, such as scratch its head, cling to the edge of the stage, grasp things and so on.

Heads for the puppets in these pictures are made from large polystyrene balls (see page 16 for directions). Each head is set on a piece of broom handle. The costume is a piece of fabric about 100 cm × 50 cm (40" × 20"). Fold fabric in half, wrong side out. Sew along the two sides, leaving openings for the neck and fingers as shown in the drawing. Sew the two corners where the fingers are to be. Turn right side out and glue or tie to rod.

This puppet has only one arm. To give it two, you will need two people.

Puppets for
Numbskull Jack

The puppets on page 91 are for Hans Christian Andersen's fairytale *Numbskull Jack*, which is on page 134. Their heads are polystyrene balls with strips of newspaper pasted on them (see page 17). They are set on round sticks with a diameter of about 12 mm ($\frac{1}{2}$").

Numbskull Jack

You will need: orange and brown fabric – felt for hands and hat – a hook-and-eye. Patterns for jacket and hands are on page 88; for hat, see page 58.

Cut the jacket in orange fabric, allowing for seams. Sew it together, leaving a neck opening large enough for a rod to go through. Turn right side out. Push the rod holding the head into the neck opening and sew up the opening.

Cut the hands from felt, not allowing for seams, oversew together in pairs, stuff with kapok and sew to the sleeves. Sew an eye to one hand, on which the crow and the clog can be hooked.

For trousers, sew two pieces of brown fabric 8 cm × 14 cm (3" × 5$\frac{1}{2}$") into two tubes. Sew tubes to front of jacket.

A rod can be sewn to one of Numbskull Jack's hands, as shown on page 93. Using papier mâché, make his clogs with tubes that can be glued into the legs. The clog he fills with mud needs no tube, but sew on a hook so that it hooks to his hand.

The goat

You will need: white teddy-bear material – beige, black, green and pink felt – brown wool – a round stick 30 cm (1') long and 12 mm ($\frac{1}{2}$") thick – card – adhesive tape – foam rubber and kapok – gauze – paste – colourless adhesive.

Cut out the parts for the goat from the patterns on pages 88–89. Make seam allowances for everything except eyes and horn.

The head Glue eyes to face and sew a black line along edge of eyelid.

Place front and back of head wrong side out, with pink felt inner mouth in between (see pages 62–63). Stitch together, leaving top of head open. Turn right side out. Stuff head, but do not overstuff mouth. Oversew beige felt horns together in pairs from right side. Stuff them and sew to sides of head. Sew together opening between horns and sew on tufts of wool as a fringe and beard. Sew ears together in pairs, wrong side out, turn right side out and sew to head.

The body Sew body pieces together, leaving bottom edge open. Sew on tuft of wool for tail. Sew head to neck as shown in drawing on the right.

Stand for the body Cover a block of foam rubber with pieces of gauze. The foam rubber must reach from the tail into the neck, about 22 cm (9") long, be about 7 cm (3") wide a

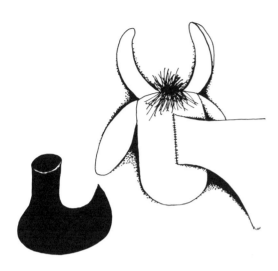

the centre, and 7 cm (3″) high at the thickest place. Make holes for two round sticks in centre of back. Make two tubes of card to fit the round sticks and glue them into the holes with a water-based adhesive.

Paste little gauze pieces all over the stand, but do not cover holes of the tubes. Glue the rod for the goat in one hole. The rod for Numbskull Jack goes through the other. You work Jack from below, making him jump up and down on the goat's back by pushing the rod up and down. Push the stand into the goat's body. Make a small opening in top back seam for Jack's rod to go through.

Numbskull Jack's clever brothers

Numbskull Jack's distinguished and well-bred brothers are made from the same patterns you used for Jack. Make them in different colours and decorate the costumes with collars, cuffs and black front panels. The collars are white felt circles with a hole in the centre for the neck. (continued on page 90)

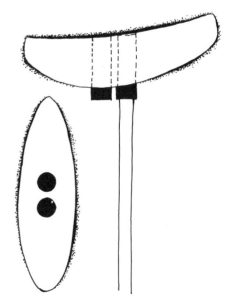

Patterns for *Numbskull Jack*

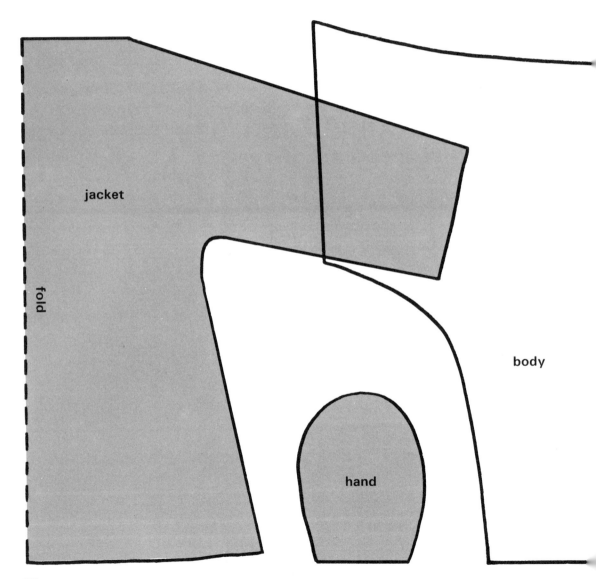

jacket

fold

body

hand

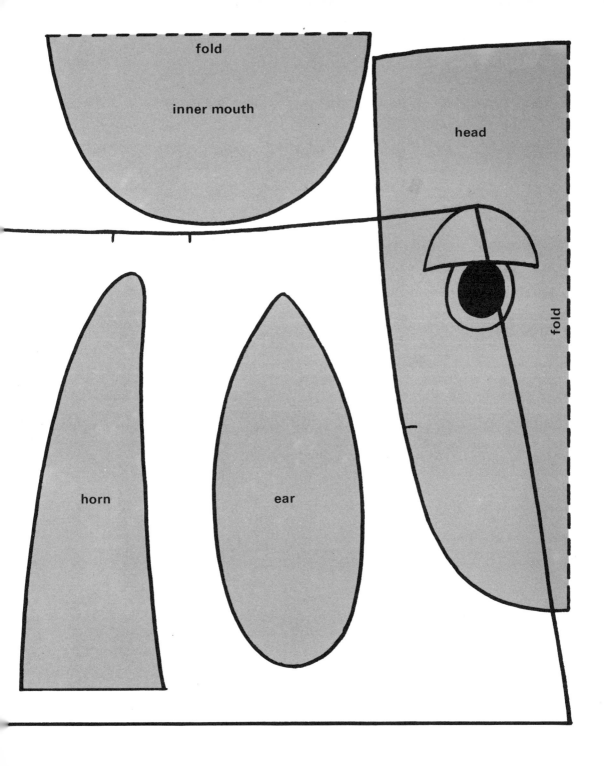

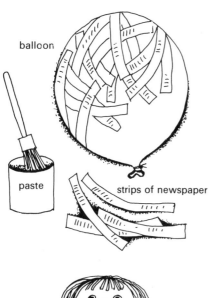

balloon

paste

strips of newspaper

Iron Vilene to the back of the collars so that it sticks out beyond the edge. Cut scallops into the Vilene.

The cuffs are made the same way, but using only half circles, folded, sewn together and sewn to the puppet's wrists.

The brothers' boots can be made like those for *The Tinder Box* (see page 36).

To make horses for the brothers, use the pattern for Numbskull Jack's goat and alter it to look like a horse.

The squire

The squire is the father of Numbskull Jack and the fashionable brothers. Make his body from papier mâché. Blow up a balloon and paste 5 layers of newspaper strips over it. When it is completely dry, burst the balloon. Cut a hole on top for the head's rod. Cut a large opening at the bottom and pull out balloon. Make a channel at edge of piece of fabric. Run a cord through the channel and glue fabric into top opening of squire's body. Tie cord round puppet's neck when rod is inserted.

Design and decorate fabric costume that will fall well down over the bulge. Glue it to the body. Make hands from fabric and glue or sew them to front of costume. Use embroidered edging for cuffs and collar.

Three musicians

The three musicians in the colour picture are rod puppets. Their bodies, heads and arms are moved by rods. Move the puppets in time with a gramophone record for a very entertaining result.

It is best to have two people to work the drummer, unless you want to beat the drum with only one stick.

You will need: dark orange, light orange, brown, pink and black felt – 4 black and 2 blue wooden beads – wool – brown fabric – one thick cotton cord – kapok – a round tin – a round stick – card – thick wire or flower sticks – 2 polystyrene balls – 2 small sticks – household glue.

Use patterns on page 96. You can make the heads as different as you wish.

The guitarist

Cut 2 guitars from dark orange felt and 2 heads from light orange felt. Allow 1 cm ($\frac{3}{8}$") for seams. Cut 4 hands from light orange felt with 0·5 cm ($\frac{1}{4}$") seam allowance, except at bottom. Cut mouth from black felt and glue it to face. Stitch a line along middle of mouth.

Place front and back of head together, wrong side out, and sew together, leaving opening at bottom. Turn right side out. Stuff head, sew on beads for eyes and frayed wool for hair. Push a round stick into head so that it nearly touches the top. Sew together opening at bottom of head on both sides of stick.

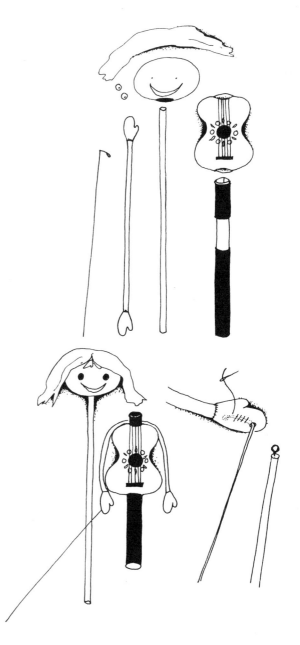

You can read about the caterpillar on page 98.

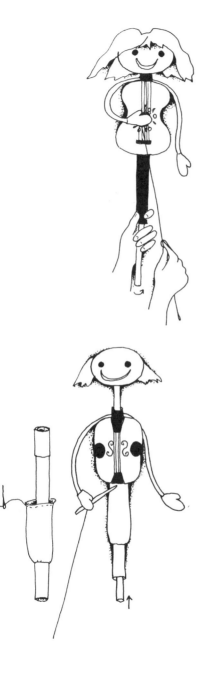

Cut felt pieces for decoration and glue to one of the guitar pieces, stitching round. The "strings" are straight rows of stitching.

Sew the two guitar pieces together, wrong side out, leaving small openings at bottom and top. Turn right side out. Stuff kapok mainly into sides, as you have to push a cardboard tube up through the guitar later. Stuff it very firmly and carefully. Make a cardboard tube to fit the round stick. It must be about 32 cm (1') long, and the stick must slide up and down in it easily. Glue a piece of black felt at top and a piece of pink felt at bottom of tube. When glue has dried, push tube into guitar. Push more kapok through openings if necessary. Sew openings together on both sides of tube. The arms are 42 cm (17") long and are made from thick cotton cord covered with brown material. Place hands together in pairs, wrong side out, and stitch together. Cut a notch in seam at thumb, then turn right side out. Fill with kapok and sew one to each end of the cord. Sew the arms to the back of the cardboard tube just above the guitar.

Use pliers to bend ends of a strong piece of wire so they will not scratch. Push wire through felt of one hand and bend it so that wire rod is at right angles to hand. Sew bent piece firmly to underside of hand. Paint rod black.

The violinist

The violinist's body and head are cut from brown felt and made the same way as the guitarist's. The tube under the violin is thicker than on the guitar. Sew a tube of pink felt a little larger than the cardboard tube. Gather bottom of felt tube round cardboard tube a little up from its lower edge. Stuff felt tube firmly and draw top edge together. Glue a piece of black felt round top and bottom of the cardboard tube. Make a bow from wood and sew it to the hand.

The drummer

Make the drum from an old tin. Make holes in the sides so that a cardboard tube can go through, as in the drawing. Glue a round piece of card to front and felt pieces to sides. The drum sticks are two polystyrene balls painted black and two small sticks painted orange. Push sticks into balls and sew to hands. The rest is made as for the guitarist.

head

fold

fold

hand

violin

fold

guitar

Patterns for caterpillar

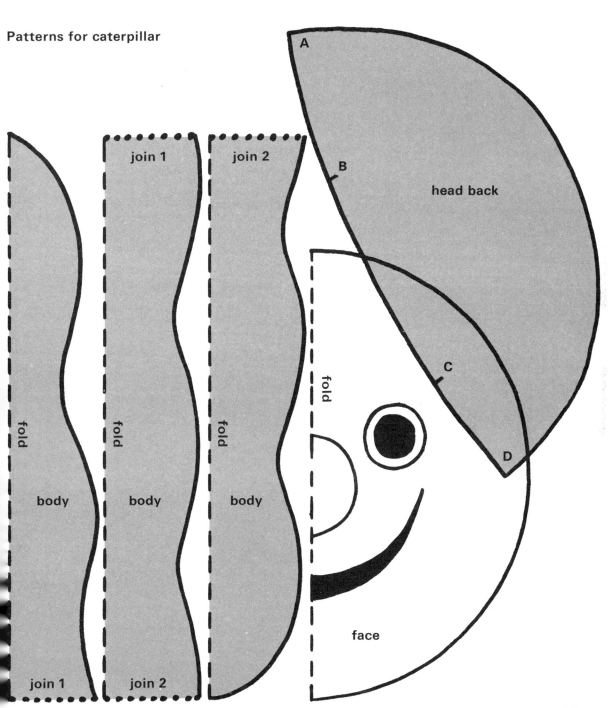

join 1

join 2

head back

A

B

C

D

fold

fold

body

fold

body

fold

body

fold

face

join 1

join 2

Caterpillar

The jolly caterpillar on page 92 is made to twist and turn by means of two rods.

You will need: about 30 cm × 60 cm (1′ × 2′) yellowish-green fabric – green wool – bits of orange, violet and white felt – 2 sequins – 2 black wooden beads – kapok – two thin round sticks – two loops.

Join ends of the three body pieces on page 97 to form a complete pattern. Cut out four complete body pieces, one face and two back heads. Allow about 1 cm ($\frac{3}{8}$″) for seams. Cut mouth from violet felt and sew it to face.

Cut pieces of wool 7 cm (3″) long and lay all round edge of face, as in drawing on right. Sew along edge of face. Place 2 backs of head together wrong side out and sew from A to B and C to D on pattern. Press seams apart and place front and back of head together wrong side out. Make sure that ends of wool still point towards centre of head. Sew together all the way round. Turn right side out.

Stuff head with kapok and sew up opening, except for 1 cm ($\frac{3}{8}$″) at bottom. A stick is pushed up here later.

For eyes, sew on two sequins and then two black wooden beads. For nose, make a ball of kapok and cut it in half. Cut a circle from orange felt and run a double draw thread along edge. Place the half ball in the centre and tighten the thread until felt fits firmly round ball. Sew it to face. Sew together the four pieces for the body and stuff with kapok. Tie green wool between the bulges.

Fix loops on two thin round sticks and sew one to head and other to tail in last but one bulge. Sew head to body.

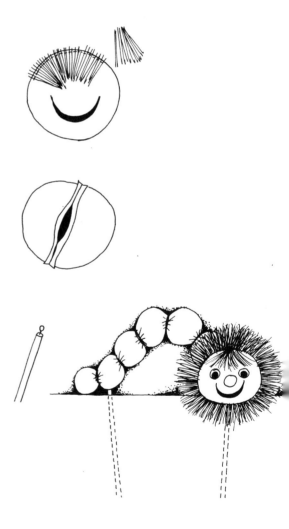

Dancing puppets

Both glove puppets and rod puppets are splendid for making up dance numbers. To make it look really good, hold the puppet with your arm stretched above your head and join in the dancing yourself.

Practise your dance until you know the movements and steps you want to use. Accompany yourself by singing or whistling, or play a record.

Dancing glove puppet
The head can be made in different ways; read about them on pages 12 to 22. The top of the costume can be cut from the pattern for the soldier's body on page 43. For the skirt, gather a straight piece of fabric to fit the waist of the top. Sew the parts together, and make a little apron, as shown in the drawing.

Dancing rod puppet
Page 78 explains how to make a very simple dancing puppet. It is rather small, but, of course, you can make it bigger. You can also make arms for it; sew them on at the top to make them swing when the puppet is dancing.

Wooden figures

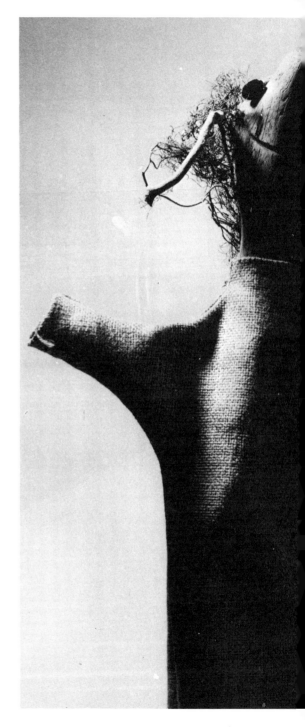

Very amusing and odd puppets can be made from driftwood, tree roots and many other things that nature provides. Perhaps you can use the things as they are, or alter them a little. You can cut, saw, sandpaper and paint them, and even glue several bits together.

The figures in the picture are dressed in a rough weave fabric that suits wood very well. Make the costumes from the pattern at the top of page 32. Make a sample costume first because you will have to adjust the pattern to the puppet's hands and head. The puppets are worked in the same way as the ghost on page 26. Holes are drilled into the heads, and rods pushed into them.

To work the puppet's hands, glue a small cardboard tube that fits your fingers around each one.

A puppet family

The puppets on page 119 are rod puppets. This is how you make them.

The owl
Sew a piece of beige fabric into a small bag, rounded at the top. Fill it with kapok and gather it together round a stick at the bottom. Sew on white felt circles and black wooden beads for eyes, and glue on a beak made of brown felt.

The man and woman
Cut out the bodies in fabric, using the pattern on pages 104–105. Sew mouth and cheeks on one piece for the woman. With fabric wrong side out, sew front and back pieces together. Leave openings at top of head and between legs. Turn right side out and push kapok into feet and arms. Sew through both layers on arms and legs along dotted lines on pattern. Push kapok into body, push stick into body between legs, and sew up opening. Glue on hair and beard. You can use buttons for eyes, and give the woman a frill round her neck. The man's pipe is cut from felt and glued on. His nose is a ball of kapok covered with material and sewn on. You can work one of the puppet arms with a rod.

102

The dog and cat

These animals are worked by two rods (you can use flower sticks). Fix a coil between the sticks. You can turn the animal's head with one stick and make it perform many funny movements. The patterns for the heads are on pages 104–105. The dog's head is sewn in the same way as the goat's on page 86. Make a small opening in rear mouth section for stick to go into head. This stick must be glued on in head. Use wooden beads for eyes, and glue a felt tongue inside the mouth.

Make cat's eyes of felt with a bead sewn on it. Embroider felt with glass beads for nose.

For the body of the cat you will need a piece of material 10 cm × 20 cm (4" × 8"), and for the dog a piece 12 cm × 16 cm (5" × 6½"). Fold fabric lengthwise and sew at sides, but not under the tummy, where there must be room for the coil to be pushed in. Make a hole at neck and push stick through. Do not glue at neck, as it must be possible to turn the head. Push in the back stick and fix coil securely inside body. If coil does not fill body, add a little kapok, but not too much. Sew body together at bottom. Glue fabric same colour as body round sticks. Make a tail from fabric-covered pipe cleaner. You can make other animals the same way too, like the lions in the drawing for example.

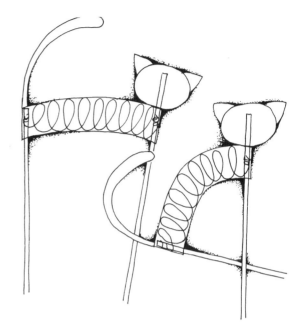

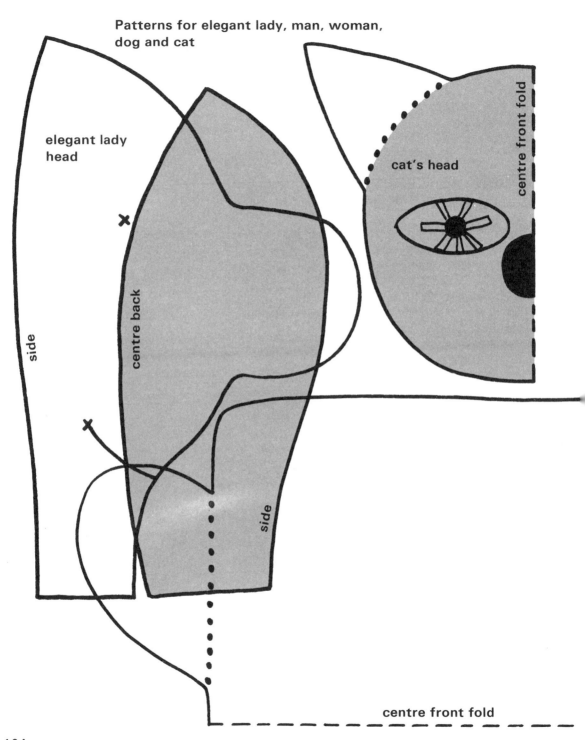

Patterns for elegant lady, man, woman, dog and cat

elegant lady head

side

centre back

X

X

side

centre front fold

cat's head

centre front fold

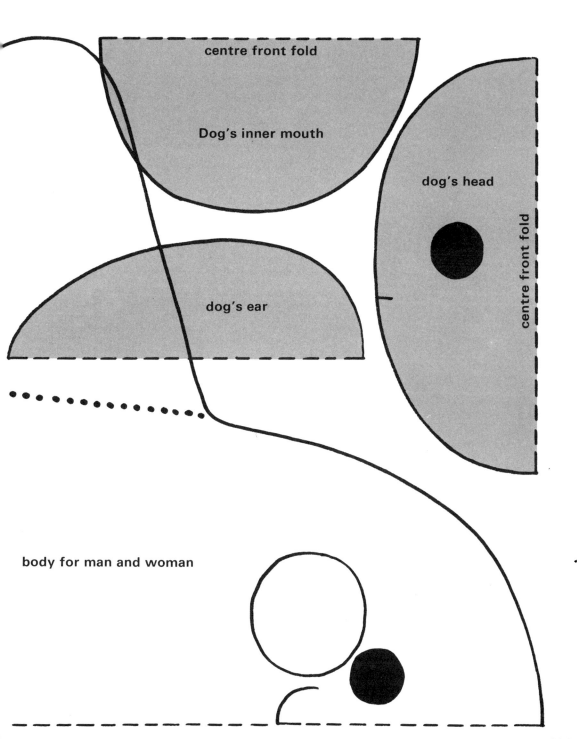

centre front fold

Dog's inner mouth

dog's head

centre front fold

dog's ear

body for man and woman

Theatres

You can put a lot of effort into making a theatre to use when you want to perform a play. But if you suddenly want to give a performance, you can make a theatre simply and quickly.

Outdoors, hang a blanket over a line stretched between two trees. Indoors, put a table on its side, lay a broom handle with blanket across it between two chairs, or hang a blanket across a door opening. Perhaps you can do without a stage and just sit facing your audience, talking to the puppets and letting them talk to the audience.

The size of the stage

Your stage must be large enough for your puppets to move about. Its size also depends on the puppets' size; tiny puppets on an enormous stage look silly — and vice versa. There must be ample room behind the stage for you and any other puppeteers, so that you do not fall over each other.

Standing, sitting or kneeling

You can stand, sit or kneel when you work puppets. The most important thing is freedom of movement. The best opportunities for working the puppets well are when you stand up with the puppets above your head. If this is too tiring, sit or kneel. If you choose to sit, it is best to use a swivel chair. You can also make an elbow-rest like the one on page 115.

Cardboard box theatre

A very simple and amusing theatre can be made from a cardboard box. Cardboard boxes of any size can be used, as long as puppets and theatre match each other in size. The theatres in the colour picture were made from cardboard boxes. If you varnish the theatre and stage sets after painting them, they will look very splendid and last a long time. It is best to paint the inside of the theatre black.

Little orange-coloured theatre

This one-man theatre is for standing on a table. It is ideal for use with little rod puppets. The back is open and you work the puppets from there. The bottom edge is just high enough to cover your hand. If you hang a black transparent cloth at the rear of the theatre, you can watch the puppets without being seen by the audience yourself.

If you glue a strip of cardboard to the back of the stage opening, you can push in various stage sets, as in the drawing.

The blue theatre

This theatre is made in the same way as the orange-coloured one, but the bottom edge is large enough to cover an arm up to the elbow. You can use glove puppets in this theatre by resting an elbow on the bottom of the box.

The boat in the picture is made from a cardboard box and fixed to the edge of the stage with a paper fastener so that it can rock. You can also make a cardboard drop curtain and push it into a groove in the top of the theatre.

A scenery theatre

We call the large theatre at the bottom a scenery theatre because the whole theatre is made like a stage set. It is meant to be used with

rod puppets like those on page 78. There is room here for two puppeteers. As in the other two theatres, the back is cut away and a piece of dark sheer fabric, called a scrim, hung up so that you can see the puppets without being seen by the audience. It is best to use a sharp hobby-knife to cut out the scenery at the front of the theatre — but mind your fingers. You can paint the cut outs and glue on coloured paper for leaves, roof tiles, stars and other decorations.

Theatre in a door opening

A door opening is ideal for a theatre. You can make a theatre very simply with a blanket hung over a broom handle. You can also make a splendid theatre from material, which can be rolled up when not in use.

The theatre in the picture opposite is made from strong cotton material. At the top there is a channel with a broom handle in it so that the theatre can be hung on a line, as in the second drawing. At the back, just below and above the edges of the stage opening, there are channels for flat strips of wood. The drawing on page 112 shows you how they are made.

The size of the theatre depends, of course, on the size of the door opening. The height of the stage opening depends on whether you want to stand, sit or kneel to use the theatre. You will have to measure these distances.

Cut out the material, leaving 5 cm (2") at the top for the channel and 8 cm (3") at the bottom for a deep hem. Allow 2 cm (1") at each side for seams. Do not cut out the stage opening yet.

Iron Vilene to the back of the fabric. It makes the theatre rigid so that it does not flap about during the performance. Sew the seams at the sides and the channel at the top. Hem

the bottom. Cut out the stage opening 3 cm ($1\frac{1}{4}$") *less* on all sides than it is to be. Cut the corners of the 3 cm ($1\frac{1}{4}$") strip on each side (see top drawing), fold the strips back and glue them to the theatre back.

Make the channels for the two strips of wood by sewing a piece of fabric to the theatre back. Make sure the channels are wide enough for the strips to be pushed in. Push in the strips and screw three small screw-eyes into the top strip — one in the centre and one at each side. This is where the drop curtain is hung.

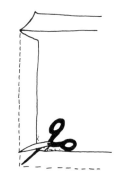

The drop curtain is made in two pieces. It must be longer and wider than the stage opening so that it covers it completely when drawn. Sew small curtain rings to the top. Place hooks in the ends of a stretch curtain rod. Push the rod through the centre eye, place the two drop curtain sections on the rod and attach the hooks to the outer eyes.

You can sew pockets below the stage, as in the picture on page 110. It can look very funny when heads suddenly appear there. There must, of course, be a hole behind the pocket for the puppets to be pushed through. You can also make round holes, as in the drawing on page 111. In this case you must hang a piece of material behind the hole.

The theatre is hung on a cord on the side of the door frame facing the audience. You can hang a backcloth on the other side of the door frame, as shown in the last drawing on the previous page.

Large theatre

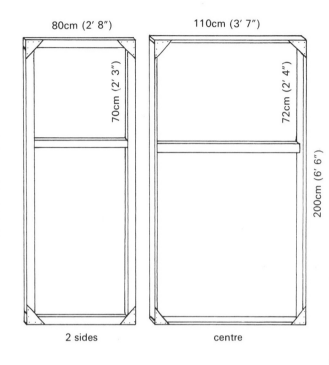

80cm (2' 8")   110cm (3' 7")

70cm (2' 3")   72cm (2' 4")

200cm (6' 6")

2 sides   centre

The photograph on page 114 shows a big puppet theatre made from wood and covered with fabric. It has three parts and takes up little space when not in use. It is easy to move about and can be used indoors and outdoors. To make only the centre section for use in a door opening, adjust these measurements to fit the door opening.

The measurements refer to the length, thickness and width of wood respectively. The number of pieces needed is in *italics*.

You will need: frames and crossbars

6 200 cm × 22 mm × 45 mm (6'6" × 1" × 2")
3 110 cm × 22 mm × 45 mm (3'7" × 1" × 2")
6 80 cm × 22 mm × 45 mm (2'8" × 1 × 2")
1 stage 110 cm × 16 mm × 110 mm
(3'7" × ¾" × 4½")
1 set holder 110 cm × 6 mm × 50 mm
(3'7" × ¼" × 2")
and 3 blocks same thickness as wood or cardboard used for scenery
3 12 cm (5") squares × 6 mm (¾")
1 round stick 160 cm (5'4") × 22 mm (1") diameter
cupboard hinges – small screw-eyes – hooks – roller blind rod and fittings – fabric – glue – nails.

Make the frame, using the drawing above as a guide. The outside measurements are given. You can change the distance to the crossbars; it depends on the height at which you want to have the stage opening. Trim the crossbars to fit inside the frames.

When you glue and nail the frames together, have the strips for the centre frame — except the crossbar — lying on their edges to give a little height. Join the side frames on the flat side. Cut the six 12 cm (5") squares in half diagonally. Nail the triangles to the corners to make the frames more rigid.

When the frames are finished, nail the stage to the crossbar on the centre frame (see drawing 3). To make a set holder on the stage, take 3 small wood blocks the same thickness as the cardboard or wood you intend to use for the sets. Nail them to the back of the stage, one in the centre and one on each side. Nail the set holder strip to the outside of

113

the blocks, flush with the back edge of the frame. This will make a groove for pushing in the scenery.

Cover the frames with material; nail it on or fix it with a strong stapling machine. You can also nail narrow pieces of wood covered with fabric at the sides and top of the stage opening. In this theatre the piece at the top is 14 cm (5½") wide and the side pieces are 8 cm (3") wide. To brace the side pieces, nail a small wood block to the stage on both sides.

Drawing 2 shows how the cupboard hinges are joined. There are two lower hinge parts on each side of the centre frame, and two top hinge parts on each side frame.

Fix three screw-eyes to the top strip of the side frames. Sew a backcloth with a channel at the top large enough for the round stick to be pushed through. Fix a bent nail at both ends of the round stick. Hang the backcloth in the screw-eyes on the side frames. This will also make the theatre nice and rigid.

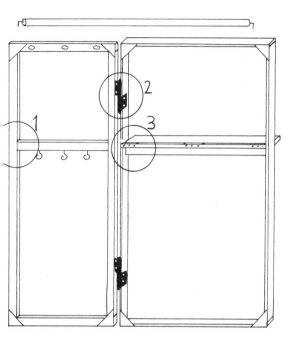

Elbow board

If you find it too tiring to work the puppets with your arms stretched, use an elbow board. Your freedom of movement is restricted, but the performance is also far less tiring. When your elbow is resting on the board, your head will come up over the edge of the stage. If you hang a piece of dark, sheer fabric in front of your face, you can see what is happening on stage, but the audience cannot see you. If you use a black backcloth and are dressed in black, you will then be completely invisible to the audience.

The elbow board can be put up with the fittings used for bookshelves.

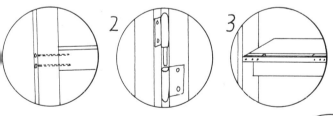

Screw small hooks for hanging the puppets on the crossbar of the side frames.

The drop curtain is made like a roller blind. Screw the fittings to the top of the side frames near the stage opening.

For lighting, use adjustable lamps fixed to the stage at each side.

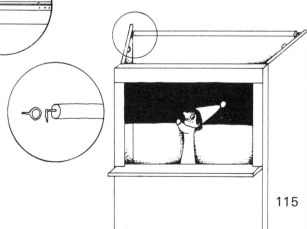

Drop curtains, props and scenery

Drop curtains

The simplest way to make drop curtains for the cardboard theatres on page 109 is from cardboard. Cut a little slit in the top of the box and push in the drop curtain there. You can either fix a stop-block to the top of the drop curtain or cut two dowels, as shown in the drawing on the left.

Fabric drop curtains can be hung with curtain rings and pulled to and fro by hand, or made like a roller blind, as on page 115.

Props

All the things the puppets need during the performance — handbags, clubs, boxes, frying pans, sausages and plates — are called props. Most of these can be made from papier mâché (see page 17). As a base, use egg trays, cardboard, pipe cleaners or other materials that will help you to get the shape you need.

For *The Fire Man* (page 143) you will need a kitchen range and a table. They can be made from small cardboard boxes. Glue a piece of cardboard to the front edge of the box so that it can stand in a groove on the stage, as shown in the bottom drawing on page 117. The range must be open at the bottom and have two holes in the top so that the Fire Man can come up through them. The chimney can be made from card and painted black like the kitchen range.

Flat scenery

The scenery should be as simple as possible — it is the puppets that must be seen. Use the scenery merely to show where the play takes place.

The drawing shows some flat scenery that can be pushed into a slit in the theatre. A glued-on cardboard stop-block prevents it from sliding too far down. You can make the scenery from cardboard or wood, and paint and varnish it. You can also make kapok relief scenery, which is described on page 121.

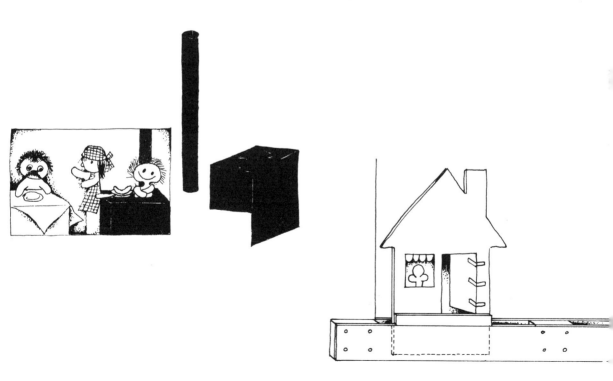

Hanging scenery

Tape small hooks made of wire or pipe cleaners to the back of the scenery. Lay a round or flat stick across your theatre above the stage opening. Now hang the scenery from the stick.

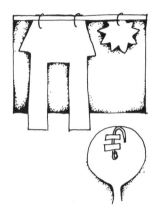

Free-hanging scenery

When you cannot hang scenery in the way described above, use Velcro tape on the back of the scenery and on the backcloth. Velcro is made of two nylon tapes, each with small spikes. The spikes interlock to hold the tapes together firmly.

   If you put black Velcro on a black felt back-cloth, for example, and on the back of a sun, a cloud, a moon, etc., you can hang the scenery pieces without using glue, and you can change the scene quickly. The castle for *The Tinder Box*, shown at the top of page 19, is fixed with Velcro tape.

Appliqué scenery

The scenery in the picture opposite is made from appliqué work. Make carboard scenery as described on page 117. Then glue material over the parts. The door in this picture was painted blue and fixed to the house by gluing on two black felt strips as hinges. The tree is covered with corduroy and has coloured Vilene leaves. Black material has been hung behind the door opening and behind the hole in the tree.

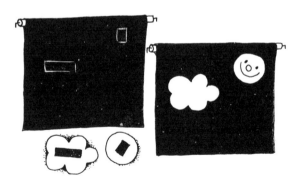

To make these puppets, see page 102.

Fluorescent theatre

The pictures on the left show four scenes from *A Moon Comedy*, which is on page 141. The puppets and scenery are made from fluorescent fabrics or painted with fluorescent paint. The stage must be lit by a special ultra-violet lamp and all other lights must be out. Then the paint and the fabrics will light up.

This is a very exciting type of theatre, but it is quite expensive — lamp, paints and fabrics cost a lot. Perhaps if there are several of you to share the costs it can be managed, and maybe you can hire the ultra-violet lamp.

To get the right effect from the fluorescent paints, everything else on stage must be black — drop curtain, backcloth and you if you appear above the edge of the stage. You must wear a black top, black gloves and a black hood. Make holes for your eyes in the hood and cover them with fine black net.

The moon, cloud and bird in the comedy are made of corrugated cardboard from a cardboard box and are worked by rods. To make them you will need: cardboard boxes – household glue – hobby knife – black and white acrylic paint – stakes – fluorescent paint.

For each character cut out two identical figures from the corrugated cardboard and glue them together. Make sure that the grooves in the cardboard are vertical so that you can push in the rod. Cut out eyes and mouth — for the moon, cut the mouth through only one piece of cardboard.

The figures can have a completely smooth surface or, as here, be made like a relief. This is done with kapok squeezed in water and dipped in paste. The paste must be kneaded well into the kapok before the kapok is placed on the cardboard, where it can be shaped as you wish. It usually takes several days to dry, but if you are impatient you can dry small items in an oven at 80°C (176°F). Large items have a tendency to buckle when they are drying.

When dry, paint the figures white on the front and black on the back with acrylic paint. Then paint the front with fluorescent paint.

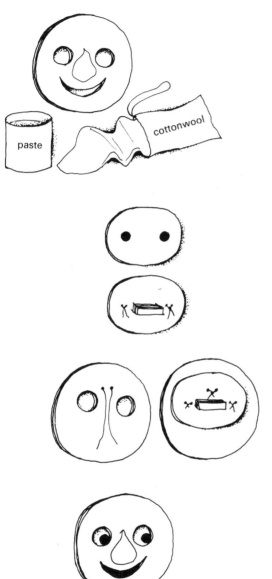

Here is how you can make movable eyes for the moon. Cut out a piece of cardboard larger than the eye sockets at the back. Paint one side with white fluorescent paint and the other side black. Sew on two black wooden beads for eyes. Push the threads through the cardboard and knot them together at the back. Glue three small bits of cardboard together to make a handle. Glue it to the back of the eye piece. Fix the piece to the moon by pulling a strong thread through it and the moon's forehead with a needle. Bring the thread ends out at the back of the piece and tie them together. The piece must fit a little loosely so that you can move it. Finally, paint handle and knots black to make the back of the moon completely black.

The spaceship lands on the cloud. Therefore, make a groove into which it can be pushed. Do this by gluing a strip of cardboard with two small pieces of cardboard in between to the back of the cloud, as shown in the drawing below.

The spaceman puts down a box on the cloud. His box can rest on a small box glued to the back of the cloud upside down.

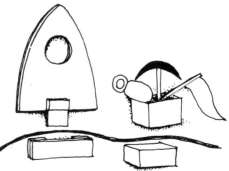

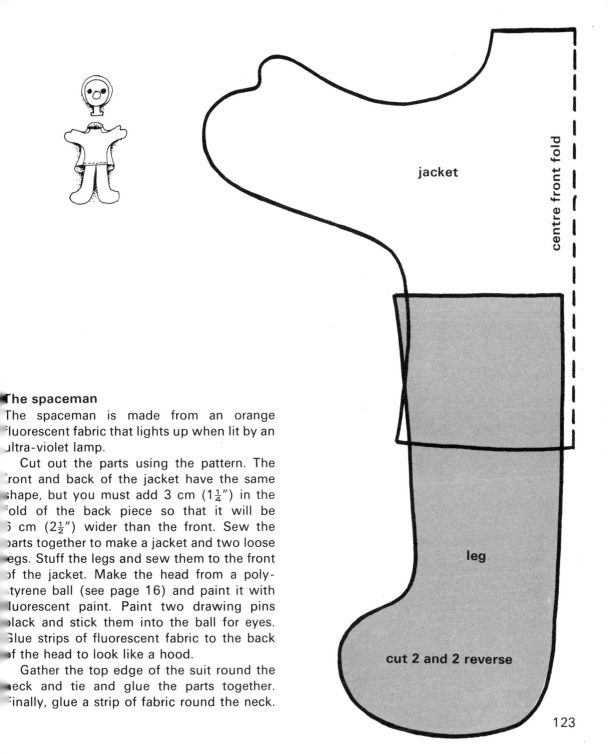

The spaceman

The spaceman is made from an orange fluorescent fabric that lights up when lit by an ultra-violet lamp.

Cut out the parts using the pattern. The front and back of the jacket have the same shape, but you must add 3 cm (1¼") in the fold of the back piece so that it will be 6 cm (2½") wider than the front. Sew the parts together to make a jacket and two loose legs. Stuff the legs and sew them to the front of the jacket. Make the head from a polystyrene ball (see page 16) and paint it with fluorescent paint. Paint two drawing pins black and stick them into the ball for eyes. Glue strips of fluorescent fabric to the back of the head to look like a hood.

Gather the top edge of the suit round the neck and tie and glue the parts together. Finally, glue a strip of fabric round the neck.

jacket

centre front fold

leg

cut 2 and 2 reverse

123

Music and sound

Your performances will probably usually have the puppets speaking or singing. You can also have performances without any speech, in which movement and sounds provide the effects. Music and sound can also be used as a background for puppets' speech to emphasize a mood. There are many ways of combining sound, music and speech, and creating sound effects. In this book only a few examples are given to inspire you to find whatever best suits your plays.

Music
A gramophone or tape recorder can be used to play the music. Perhaps you can make up a play in which the music is the most important part, by having the puppets acting as opera singers, for example, or by making them dance to the music.

Musical instruments
Make the music yourself by playing an instrument. Almost any instrument can be used. You can make your own instrument.

Drum
Turn a bucket upside down and beat it with wooden spoons or sticks with the ends covered in material.

Maracas

Put dried peas or rice in 2 empty yoghurt beakers and tape the beakers together.

Rhythm instrument

Beat two wooden spoons together.

Saucepan lids

Beat two saucepan lids against each other in time with the music.

Bottles with water

Pour varying amounts of water into bottles; the more water in the bottle, the higher the note. A complete scale can be made in this way. Hang bottles on strings along a broom handle resting across two chairs; hit them with a wooden spoon.

Comb

Place a piece of greaseproof paper round a comb and sing with the lips tight against the paper.

Elastic band instrument

Stretch some elastic bands around an empty box and pluck them as strings.

Sound effects

You can buy records with various sounds, birds twittering, rain, horses' hooves, etc., but you can also make many sounds yourself with very simple means. Here are a few examples.

Bird-song

Whistle or play a recorder.

Roaring sea and rain
Pour dried peas or lentils into a plastic dish. Swing them round in the dish more or less violently.

Thunder
Shake a metal plate or big piece of card.

Windy weather
Blow with varying strength. If you have a tape recorder, blow into the microphone.

Streams or waterfalls
Pour water from a jug into a bowl.

Shots
Beat a ruler hard on a table, use a toy revolver with caps, or blow up a paper bag and burst it.

Horses' hooves
Drum a table top with your fingers. Vary the sound by using different underlays, such as fabric or cardboard. Put thimbles on your fingers to make the sound stronger.

Noise-making instruments
Use rattles, toy trumpets, whistles, combs, alarm clocks and bells.

Tape recording
Instead of speaking while you work the puppets, you can record the entire performance beforehand on tape and play it while you move the puppets. You can also record the sound effects and perhaps get some surprising effects — driving cars, animal sounds, factory whistles, sirens, and aeroplanes, for example.

To work puppets in time with a tape is, however, much more difficult than you think and needs a lot of practice. When you are recording the tape you must bear in mind the time you need to put on the puppets, bring them on the stage, take them off it, change puppets, etc. Therefore, you must have suitable intervals on the tape. Also remember that the room in which you are recording must be completely silent. You will be very surprised at the amount of noise picked up from chairs being moved and the din from the street. The puppets speaking on the tape must, of course, be on stage when they speak, and if a dog is supposed to bark, it is wrong for a horse in the play to open its mouth instead.

Lighting

If you have made a fine puppet theatre and some good puppets it is worth making an effort to be sure that the audience can see what is happening on the stage. If you are performing out-of-doors during the day, you will not need artificial light, but in the evening it is essential.

If you are performing on a table with a lamp above it, use the lamp to throw light down on the puppets. If you are performing in a door opening or in your own theatre, you will have to arrange the lighting. A draughtsman's lamp or two fixed to the theatre or on a couple of chairs in front of it is an excellent solution. But they must be adjusted so that they light up the puppets absolutely correctly. They must not light up your face. Place the lamps at the sides pointing towards the centre of the stage. Create different moods by varying the light. Only one lamp on one side creates contrasts and shadows on the stage, whereas light from both sides evens out the shadows. Lighting from below gives an eerie atmosphere.

Scenery can also be lit from behind the stage. The picture on page 119 shows the important part lighting can play. A lamp has been placed on each side behind the stage. The one on the left lights up leaves and feathers; the one on the right lights up the background of the cat to give the cat almost the effect of a silhouette. Another lamp illuminates the puppets from the front of the stage.

You can also use torches and bicycle lamps to give a light behind windows.

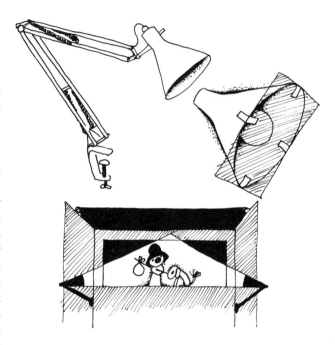

Coloured lighting

Coloured cellophane taped to the front of a lamp produces an exciting effect. If you use red cellophane, for example, the figures will, of course, become reddish, but the shadows will not be black — they will be green. Different coloured cellophane produces shadows in other colours.

127

Plays

Funny Face and Sour Head

Plays can be made up in many different ways. You can think up a play yourself, and either write down the dialogue or make it up as you go along. You can also adapt a story into a play. This book gives some ideas that may inspire you.

Thomas, aged 6, made up a little play with the two puppets on the cover of the book. He calls the happy puppet Funny Face and the grumpy puppet Sour Head. You can make up a play with your puppets too. It is not necessary to make up a play with a lot happening. The movements of the puppets and what they say is often enough in itself.

To perform *Funny Face and Sour Head,* you will need the puppets and a lemon.

(Sour Head comes onstage.)
Sour Head: Hello. My name's Sour Head. It's a jolly rotten name. I got it because I'm always sour. And that's not very nice either.

(Funny Face comes onstage.)
Funny Face: Hello! My name's Funny Face. Isn't that funny?
Sour Head: What's funny about it?
Funny Face: Well, it's a funny name. Let's play something.
Sour Head: What shall we play?
Funny Face: We can go to the playground and go on the swings.
Sour Head: I'll only get the swings hitting me on the head.
Funny Face: Then we could play in the sandpit.
Sour Head: Bah! That'll be messy.
Funny Face: Then let's slide down the slide.
Sour Head: I'll hurt myself.
Funny Face: What else can we do?
Sour Head: Well, we could let the air out of the tyres of some bikes.
Funny Face: Fine! We'll let the air out of the tyres of your bike.
Sour Head: Ooh! It's always me that gets treated badly (weeps)! Besides, the weather's awful. It's raining.
Funny Face: That's fun! We can walk in the rain.
Sour Head: It's not fun at all! Anyway, it's not raining now; the sun's shining and we'll get fried.
Funny Face: Well, that's fun!
Sour Head: No, it's not fun at all! Besides, it's started snowing.
Funny Face: Well, that's fun! We can build snowmen.

Sour Head: I don't like that. And it's stopped snowing — there's a gale blowing.

Funny Face: Well, that's fun!

Sour Head: No, that's no fun at all!

Funny Face: Why are you always so sour?

Sour Head: I think it's because I once ate a lemon — with peel on — the lot. It's lying in my tummy.

Funny Face: Shall I help you to get it out?

Sour Head: You won't be able to. It's lying right at the bottom of my tummy. (Funny Face bends down below the edge of the stage in front of Sour Head.)

Funny Face: Yes, I've got it! Here it is! (He lifts up the lemon.)

Sour Head: My! A lemon! I love lemons. Takes the lemon and to the audience it looks as if he is eating it.) Phew! Ugh! That was horrible! I can't stand lemons and now I've swallowed it. It's lying in my tummy.

Funny Face: I'll get it out again. (He bends down in front of Sour Head and takes out the lemon.) Here it is. But you're not going to eat again. (Puts it away.)

Sour Head: I'm still sour. And — hic — now I've got the — hic — hiccups.

Funny Face: Why are you still sour?

Sour Head: Because I've got the — hic — hiccups — hic. You'll — hic — have to help me. You'll have — hic — to frighten — hic — me.

Funny Face: (shouts) Boo!

Sour Head: Oh! You frightened me. Never do that again!

Funny Face: (shouts) Boo!

Sour Head: Oh! You've frightened me again. Why do you keep on doing that?

Funny Face: To make you stop hiccupping.

Sour Head: Well, is that so? Hic!

Funny Face: (shouts) Boo! Boo!

Sour Head: Oh no! You're doing it again. But I'm not hiccupping any more. Do you hear? I'm not hiccupping any more.

Funny Face: Hic!

Sour Head: (shouts) Boo!

Funny Face: Oh! Now you've frightened me — hic!

Sour Head: (shouts) Boo! Boo!

Funny Face: Well, I'm not hiccupping any more either.

Sour Head: I'm still sour. I'm very sour.

Funny Face: Now I'm tickling you (tickles Sour Head).

Sour Head: Now I'm not sour any more! Stop it! I'm not a bit sour any more. Ooh! How it tickles!

Make a play from a book

If you want to try something other than writing your own plays, you might try to make a story or part of a book into a play. You can start with a strip cartoon and make your puppets represent the figures in it. Very few stories can be used as they are. In most cases you will have to make up new dialogue yourself. Do this in advance and write it down. You can also make up things to say as you go along. It is not very difficult if you have practised a couple of times. The important thing is that the stories should be suitable for puppet theatres. If, for example, a story needs many changes of scenery you may have to simplify it.

Here is a suggestion of how to do it. We have used a book called *Albert*, by Ole Lund Kirkegaard. Albert is a bright little boy who has lots of adventures. This is how Albert is described in the book: "His hair bristled out like a broom, and his eyes were hidden behind greasy, round glasses, which his mother had to patch up with sticking plaster because Albert broke them every time he fell out of a pear tree." The section we have used is about Albert, the farmer, and Big Peter, who is much taller than Albert.

The scene

In the foreground to one side make a hedge out of painted cardboard. The puppets have to come up in front of, and behind, the hedge. Behind the hedge is the farmer's garden. In it a pear tree, which you can also make from cardboard. In the background, perhaps on the backcloth, is a hen house. You will also need radishes made of cardboard or Plasticine. The audience doesn't have to see them growing in the garden. When Albert pulls them up, he can just bend down and you give them to him with your free hand.

The play

Albert is sitting at the front of the stage looking through the hedge into the farmer's garden. He is looking at the pear tree. Big Peter appears.

Big Peter: Well, well! Here is one of those silly little boys who have nothing but porridge in their heads. (Albert is frightened.) If you are brave enough to climb into that garden and pull some radishes out of the ground I won't beat you up.

Albert: What on earth are radishes?

Big Peter: Bah! Didn't I say you were small and stupid? Can't you see the green leaves sticking up out of the ground in that garden?

Albert: Yes. Are they radishes?

Big Peter: You bet your life they are! If you pull at the green leaves the radishes will come up out of the ground.

Albert: Well, that's easy! (Albert walks into the garden and Big Peter hides behind the hedge. Albert pulls out the radishes.) My! There's nothing to it.

Big Peter: Then pull out a few more. (Albert pulls up more radishes.)

Albert: My! I'm clever at a lot of things! (The farmer comes rushing onstage swinging a stick.)

Farmer (shouts): I'll teach a little layabout like you to pull up radishes in my garden!

Albert: My goodness! What an angry man! I think I'd better climb a tree.

(Albert climbs the pear tree, and Big Peter disappears.)

Farmer: I've never seen anything like it! First you pull up my radishes and now you're climbing my best pear tree.

Albert: What! Is this really a pear tree?

Farmer: I'll stay here until you come down. And then I'm going to give you a jolly good hiding.

Albert: Perhaps he'll cool down if I talk to him nicely. I'll try asking him a question. Hey! Do you want some of my toy bricks?

Farmer: Now you're going too far. You're not only a little horror, ruining people's gardens, but you're cheeky as well!

Albert: Perhaps you don't play with bricks? (The farmer is furious.) Bah! He's not easy to talk to. (Albert catches sight of the hen house.) Is that your hen house?

Farmer: You bet it is!

Albert: Are dogs allowed in there?

Farmer: WHAT! That's the worst thing that can happen. Next to boys, dogs are the worst things I know.

Albert: Well, I'm almost sure I saw a very big dog go in there.

Farmer: WHAT! A dog in my hen house! (The farmer hurries to the hen house, looks in, but doesn't see any dog. Meanwhile, Albert climbs down from the tree and dashes out. The farmer turns towards the tree.) What a rascal! Never in my life have I known such a cheeky little rascal.

The Tinder Box

The Tinder Box is a fairytale by Hans Christian Andersen. It is very suitable for a puppet theatre. Directions for making the puppets start on page 34. Here is the story. There is not much dialogue—try to think up some more for your play.

A soldier is marching along the road. He meets an old witch who asks him if he would like a huge amount of money. Of course the soldier would like that!

"Then go down into that hollow tree," says the witch. "At the bottom of the tree are three small rooms. In the first room is a box full of copper coins and a dog with eyes as big as teacups. Move the dog and take all the money you want. In the next room is a box full of silver coins and a dog with eyes as big as mill wheels. Move the dog and take all the silver you want. In the third room is a box full of gold coins and a dog with eyes as big as the Round Tower in Copenhagen, but just move him aside. Then take all the gold you want. All I want is an old tinder box my grandmother left in the tree."

The soldier ties a rope round his waist and climbs down into the tree. He goes into the first room, moves the dog and fills his pockets with copper coins. In the second room he moves the dog, throws away the copper coins and fills his pockets with silver. In the last room he moves the dog, throws away the silver and fills his pockets with gold.

"Now hoist me up, witch!" he shouts.

"Have you got the tinder box?" she asks.

"No, I forgot it," says the soldier, and goes back to fetch it. When he has come up out of the tree he asks the witch what she wants with the tinder box. She will not tell him. "Then I'll cut off your head," says the soldier — and he does.

Arriving in a town, the soldier goes to a fine hotel and begins spending his money. He hears about the beautiful princess whom no one is allowed to see because it has been foretold that she will marry an ordinary soldier.

One day the soldier has no money left and has to move into a small attic room. Sitting in his room, he strikes a light with the tinder box and — presto! — the dog with eyes as big as teacups appears.

"What is my master's wish?" he asks.

"Can you get me some money?" asks the soldier. The dog returns with some money. "What a tinder box!" says the soldier. Then he decides he would like to see the beautiful princess. He strikes the tinder box twice and the second dog appears. The soldier asks him to fetch the princess. The dog goes and returns with the sleeping princess. The soldier gives her a kiss and the dog takes her back to the castle. She is still asleep.

The next day the princess tells the king and queen that she dreamt she was taken away by a dog and kissed by a soldier. A lady-in-waiting is ordered to watch by her bed. That night the lady-in-waiting sees the dog carrying away the princess. She runs after it and paints a cross on the door of the house it enters. But when the dog goes to return the princess, he paints crosses on all the doors in town so that the courtiers cannot find where the soldier is living.

The next night the queen sews a bag of fine grain on the princess's gown and cuts a hole in it. When the dog runs off with the princess, the grain runs out of the bag and the courtiers follow the trail to the soldier. He is thrown in prison and is about to be hanged. He sends a boy to fetch his tinder box.

When the soldier is brought to the gallows he asks for a last wish — a pipe of tobacco. This is granted. He strikes the tinder box and the three dogs appear. They throw the judges, the king and queen into the air. The people are very happy and declare the soldier their king. So he becomes king and, of course, marries the beautiful princess.

To simplify the play for your puppet theatre, leave out some scene changes. For example, divide the story like this.

Scene 1: At the tree
Instead of changing scenery when the soldier climbs down into the tree, just make him shout to the witch above, ''Now I can see the dog with eyes as big as teacups,'' etc. Emphasize the words by jingling coins, creaking doors, etc.

Scene 2: At the hotel
To show the difference between the splendid suite and the poor attic, change the scenery or the backcloth.

Scene 3: At the castle
After the princess has told about her dream the play can take place in the castle. The courtiers can report all the action, how they ran after the dog, saw crosses on all the doors, followed the trail of grain and found the soldier.

Scene 4: At the town square
While things are being made ready for the hanging, the soldier can be shown sitting behind scenery or a backcloth made like a prison wall, looking out of a window.

Numbskull Jack

Directions for making the puppets for Hans Christian Andersen's fairytale *Numbskull Jack* begin on page 86. The fairytale contains so much dialogue that you can almost use it as it is, or you can make up new dialogue yourself.

The play can be divided into three scenes: at the squire's home, on the way to the castle and in the great hall of the castle.

There are many ways to make the scenery interesting. For example, the red-hot pipe on the stove at the castle can be made from red paper. Put a torch behind it to make it glow.

In the country there was an old farm and in it lived an old squire. He had two sons who were so clever that half of it would have been enough. They wanted to ask for the king's daughter's hand in marriage. She had let it be known that she would marry the man whom she found could best speak up for himself.

Now the two brothers took eight days preparing themselves, which was the time allowed for this. It was quite enough, for they were well-educated, which, of course, is most useful. One brother knew by heart the entire Latin dictionary and the town's newspaper for the last three years, and both forwards and backwards at that! The other brother knew all the by-laws of the city and what every alderman ought to know if he wanted to talk about politics — or what he thought he should know. He also knew something about embroidering braces and belts, for he was smart and nimble with his hands.

"I'll win the king's daughter!" they both said. Their father gave them each a wonderful horse. Then the brothers rubbed the corners of their lips with codliver oil so that the words would come out smoothly. All the servants watched them mount their horses in the courtyard. Just then the third brother arrived. There were three brothers, but nobody counted him as one because he was not as clever as the other two. He was called Numbskull Jack. "Where are you off to?" he asked.

"To Court to talk to the king's daughter. Haven't you heard what everyone is talking about?" And then they told him.

"My word! I'd better come too," said Numbskull Jack. His brothers laughed at him and rode away.

"Father, give me a horse!" cried Jack. "I want to marry the king's daughter."

"I'm not giving you a horse," said his father. "You can't talk properly, but your brothers are clever fellows."

"I'll take the goat," said Numbskull Jack. "It's my very own and quite fit to carry me." He sprawled astride the goat and rode quickly down the road.

The brothers were riding ahead quietly. They were thinking about all the fine things they were going to say, for it had to be ever so clever.

"Hello!" shouted Numbskull Jack. "Look what I found on the road," and he showed them a dead crow.

"Numbskull!" they said. "What do you want with that?"

"I'm going to give it to the princess."

"A good idea," they laughed, and rode ahead of him.

"Hello! Look what I found this time."

The brothers stopped and looked. "Numbskull!" they said. "It's an old clog that's lost its upper. Is that for the king's daughter too?"

"Certainly," said Numbskull Jack. The brothers laughed and rode off far ahead.

"Hello! Here I come," cried Jack again.

"What have you found this time?" the brothers asked.

"Well," said Numbskull Jack, "I just can't describe it. How pleased the king's daughter will be."

"Bah!" said the brothers, "it's nothing but mud straight out of the ditch."

"So it is," said Jack. "It's the very finest sort; so fine you can't hold on to it."

The clever brothers rode on and arrived at the city gate a whole hour before Jack. Here the suitors were arranged in rows, so close together they couldn't move their arms. All the other people in the country were standing round the castle peering in through the windows to see the princess receive her suitors. No sooner did a suitor enter the room than he became tongue-tied.

"No good," said the king's daughter each time. "Out!"

An alderman stood at one side of the room and at each window there were three clerks, who wrote down everything that was said so that it could go straight into the newspaper to be sold on the corner. What's more, the stove was stoked up so much that the pipe was red hot.

Now the brother who knew the dictionary appeared, but he had completely forgotten it while he was standing in the queue.

"It's horribly hot in here," he said.

"That's because my father is roasting a chicken," said the king's daughter.

"Oh." He hadn't expected this kind of talk. He wanted to say something, but he couldn't think of a word.

"No good," said the princess. "Out!"

Now the second clever brother appeared. "The heat in here is dreadful," he said.

"Yes, we're roasting a chicken today," said the king's daughter.

"B-b-beg pardon?" he said. All the clerks wrote down "B-b-beg pardon."

"No good," said the princess. "Out!"

Now Numbskull Jack appeared. He rode his goat right into the room. "Goodness, it's as hot as the devil in here," he said.

"I'm roasting a chicken," said the king's daughter.

"Jolly good," said Numbskull Jack, "perhaps I can roast my crow too."

"Of course," said the princess. "But have you got something to roast it in? I haven't got a pot or pan to spare."

"You bet I have!" said Jack. He pulled out the old clog and put the crow in it.

"That will make quite a meal," said the princess, "but what about the gravy?"

"I've got that right here," Numbskull Jack said. And he poured a little mud out of his pocket and into the clog.

"I like that," said the king's daughter. "You, at least, can speak up and give me an answer. You're the one I want for my husband. But do you know that every word we've said has been written down and will be in the newspaper tomorrow? You'll see three clerks at each window, and an old alderman. The alderman is the worst — he understands absolutely nothing." She said this to frighten Jack, and all the clerks giggled.

"Then I'll have to give the alderman one in the eye," said Numbskull Jack. And he turned and threw mud in the alderman's face.

"Well done!" said the king's daughter. "I couldn't have done it better myself."

So Numbskull Jack became king, got a wife and a crown and sat upon a throne, and this we have read in the alderman's newspaper — but that's not too reliable.

The Ugly Duckling

The Ugly Duckling is also a fairytale by Hans Christian Andersen. It can be made into a puppet play in many different ways. You can make fine scenery or you can do without scenery altogether. You can make hand puppets with movable mouths (see page 71) or rod puppets from corrugated cardboard (see page 80).

We have shortened the story a little and suggested how to divide the play into scenes. Perhaps you can make up some more dialogue.

Scene 1

Mother Duck is sitting on her eggs and the ducklings appear one by one. One egg is larger than the others. No duckling appears out of it. (The eggs can be made from cardboard and painted white on the side facing the audience. Let the chicks come up from behind the eggs.)

An old duck comes up to Mother Duck.

Old duck: Well, how's it going?

Mother Duck: This one egg takes so long. It just won't crack. But have a look at the others. They are the most delightful ducklings I've ever seen. They all look like their father.

Old duck: Let me see the egg that won't crack. It's a turkey's egg for sure. I was cheated like that once. I had my worries and troubles with those youngsters, because they're afraid of water. I couldn't get them in. I quacked and snapped, but little did that help. Yes, that's a turkey's egg. Leave it alone and teach the other children to swim.

Mother Duck: No, I want to sit on it a little longer. I've been sitting for so long that it won't make any difference to sit a bit longer.

Old duck: Please yourself.

(The old duck goes away. At last a duckling appears from the big egg — a big duckling.)

Mother Duck: What an enormous duckling! None of the others looks like this. I wonder whether it really is a turkey chick. Well, we'll soon find out. Into the water he goes — even if I have to kick him in!

Mother Duck comes up to the front of the stage, and the ducklings jump into the water one by one. (Make the puppets hop once and then make gliding movements at the back of the stage to make it look as if they are swimming.) The big duckling jumps in last and swims about grandly among the others.

Mother Duck: No, that's no turkey. Look how wonderfully it uses its legs and how straight it carries itself. It's my very own duckling. It's really quite beautiful if you look at it carefully. Quack, quack! Come with me; I'll lead you out into the world and introduce you all to the duck-yard. Always stay near me so that nobody steps on you. And look out for the cats!

Scene 2

In the duck-yard. There are various animals in the duck-yard; an old duck with a red rag tied round one leg, some young ducks and a cock. Mother Duck enters with the ducklings.

Mother Duck: Now use your legs! Hurry up with you, and bend your necks to the old duck over there. She's the most distinguished duck here. You see that red rag round her leg. That's the highest honour a duck can have. It means that no one would even think of doing away with her, and that she must be recognised by man and beast. Hurry up and don't turn your toes in! A well-mannered duckling walks with its legs wide apart. Like this. Nod your head and say "Quack"!

One of the ducks: Ugh, what a sight that big duckling is! We won't stand him. (He bites the big duckling.)

Mother Duck: Leave him alone. He isn't doing anything.

Duck: No, but he's too big and he looks strange.

Old duck with rag round her leg: This lady has some beautiful children. All of them are beautiful except that one. I wish you could make him all over again.

Mother Duck: That's impossible, Your Grace. He isn't beautiful, but he's very good-natured. He swims as beautifully as any of the others; yes, perhaps even better. I think he will grow up to be beautiful or get a bit smaller as time goes by. He's been in the egg too long; that's why he didn't get the right shape. Besides, he's a drake, and it doesn't matter so much. He'll manage all right.

Old duck: Well, the other ducklings are nice. Make yourself at home.

But the other ducks tease and peck the big duckling. "He's too big," they say. "If only the cat would grab you, you ugly monster." "If only you weren't here." The big duckling becomes so unhappy that it runs out of the duck-yard — and off the stage.

Scene 3

The big duckling is lying exhausted across the edge of the stage. Two wild ducks come flying in.

Wild ducks: Whatever are you? (The duckling greets the two wild ducks with surprise.) You're terribly ugly, but we don't mind as long as you don't marry into our family.

The wild ducks fly off and the duckling is left lying there very unhappy.

Two wild geese come flying in.

One of the wild geese: Hello, old chap! You're so ugly that I quite like you. Would you like to come along with us and be a migratory bird? Not far away, in another marsh, there are some heavenly wild geese — all of them girls.

There is the sound of two shots (burst two paper bags or fire a toy pistol), and the wild geese collapse. A big dog appears on the stage, growls at the ugly duckling and takes off the two dead wild geese.

The duckling: I'm so ugly that even the dog can't bring himself to bite me.

It lies there quiet and sad, then gets up and slowly leaves the stage.

Scene 4

In a farm house. There is a cat, a hen and an old woman. The ugly duckling sneaks into the room and hides as well as it can. At last the woman catches sight of him.

Woman: What have we here? A good fat duck. That was a good catch. Now I can get some duck's eggs. If only it isn't a drake. We'll have to see. (She puts the duck on the front of the stage.)

Hen to the Duckling: Can you lay eggs?

Duckling: No.

Hen: Well then, be quiet.

Cat: Can you arch your back and purr?

Duckling: No.

Cat: Well then, you're not much use.

The duckling sits quietly for a long time.

Duckling: When I see the clear air outside and the sunshine I feel I want to swim.

Hen: You've nothing to do, that's why you get these fancies. Lay some eggs or purr, then it'll pass away.

Duckling: But it's so wonderful to swim in the water. It's marvellous to put your head under the water and to dive to the bottom.

Hen: Have you gone mad? Ask the cat — he's the wisest I know — whether he would like to swim in the water or to dive. I won't talk about myself. You ask our mistress, the old woman. There's no one wiser than her in the whole world. Do you think she wants to swim around and put her head under the water?

Duckling: You won't understand me.

Hen: Well, if *we* don't understand you, who on earth *will*? Don't pretend that you're wiser than the cat and the woman, let alone me. Don't be a fool. Thank heaven for your good luck. Haven't you come into a warm room among people who will teach you something? But you talk nonsense. Believe you me, I want to help you. I say unkind things to you and that's how you can tell who are your real friends. Now get on with laying eggs or learn to purr.

Duckling: I think I want to go out into the wide world.

Hen: Go ahead!

The duckling walks away.

Scene 5

The duckling swims around, and now and then lays its head mournfully across the edge of the stage. Then it swims around again and finally swims off the stage.

Scene 6

Two swans are swimming around. Then a third swan comes on the stage. This is the ugly duckling; he has become a swan, but doesn't know it.

Duckling: I'm going to join them, those royal birds, and they'll peck me to death because I, who am so ugly, dare to approach them. But it doesn't matter. Rather be killed by them than nipped by the ducks, pecked by the hens, kicked by the maid who looks after the hens, and suffer hardship during the winter. (It swims towards the swans.) Go ahead and kill me! (The duckling bends its head, sees its reflection in the water and discovers that it is a swan itself.) Look! I'm no longer a clumsy, ugly duckling. I'm a swan! I'm a swan!

The other swans swim up to it and stroke it with their beaks. A boy comes up to the front of the stage.

Boy: There's a new swan, and it's the most beautiful of all.

A Moon Comedy

make the puppets. It's not necessary to make the scenery and puppets using fluorescent materials that need a special lamp. Instead, you can use ordinary materials and paints.

1 On the stage, which has a completely black drop curtain and backcloth, a cloud is seen. It is set a little back from the front edge, as the bird and the spaceship must be able to fly round it. The cloud can be made with two rods tied to the back of a chair. You can make some sound for the cloud, such as whistling.

2 A hand slowly appears. First we see its fingers creeping up over the edge of the cloud and holding on to it. Gradually it becomes more daring and eventually comes up quite clear of the cloud. The sound for the hand can be a triangle. Beat it in time with the movements of the hand. The whistling for the cloud continues.

3 The hand again grasps the top edge of the cloud. Slowly a shy moon peeps up over the cloud's edge. As soon as it sees the audience it ducks down again quickly. It tries looking up again and rolls its eyes all the way round as if to see whether it dares to come right out. Finally it plucks up courage and comes right up. It scratches its head, turns from side to side and right around. As it is flat, when it is turning it will look like the moon itself as it waxes and wanes. It turns its front toward the audience. It moves to and fro along the cloud, and perhaps dances a bit. The sound of whistling can stop now. Try to find sounds for the moon yourself. You may use an instrument to make the sound, or you may want to speak gibberish. Whatever you choose, the

You can make up plays without any words, using only sounds and the movements of the puppets as effects. As an example, here is *A Moon Comedy*.

In the play there are a cloud, a moon with a "loose" hand, a bird, a spaceship and a spaceman. Pages 121–123 show how to

tone must represent the moon's moods. First it is bashful and a little afraid, then it becomes braver, and finally it turns round and dances across the cloud.

4 A little later an excited twittering of birds is heard in the distance. This can be a recorder or — if you use a tape recorder — a tape with speech running backwards. The moon's eyes follow the sound and use the hand to beckon whoever is making the sound to come closer.

5 A bird appears and flies round and round the moon excitedly, twittering all the time. At last it lands on the cloud and talks to the moon. A humming noise is heard far away (this noise can be made with a comb and paper). It comes nearer and nearer. The bird gets very excited and rushes off the stage in the opposite direction to its entrance.

6 The reason for all the excitement now appears on the stage; a spaceship. It circles round the moon a couple of times and then lands on the cloud beside the moon, which looks on with rolling eyes and moves a little to one side. When the spaceship has landed, the humming noise stops. A spaceman gets out of the spaceship. He jumps up and down a little with slow movements, just like the astronauts do. Then he fetches a box from the ship. There are various tools in the box, such as a pickaxe, a spade and a drill. There is also a flag. He places the box on the cloud. While this has been going on, the moon has followed the spaceman's movements, thoughtfully scratched its head, held its chin and rocked its head from side to side. Now it stretches

out its hand to the spaceman to welcome him. The spaceman nods and waves his arms. The moon does not understand this, but waits to see what will happen.

7 The spaceman starts to examine the moon. He looks at its mouth, nose and eyes, goes round it and behind it, and re-appears on top of its head. The moon's eyes still follow what is happening. The man stands still for a moment looking at the moon, then climbs down to fetch a pickaxe. When he returns he begins to pick at the top of the moon's head. At each blow a drum or something similar is beaten, and the moon sinks down behind the cloud in time with the blows. At last it is right down and the man is level with the cloud. He walks up to his box, puts down the pickaxe and takes out a drill. Meanwhile, the moon has come up again. The man climbs on top of it and begins to drill into the moon's head. Loud drilling noises are heard.

8 The moon is tired of all this fooling about with its head, and to get rid of the man it slowly turns round. It becomes smaller and smaller, and finally the man is balancing on the tip of the moon. Then he falls down on the cloud with a good smack; the moon has now disappeared completely, because its black back cannot be seen by the audience. The man gathers up his tools, rushes to the spaceship and flies away. Humming noises are heard again.

The Fire Man

The action takes place in a kitchen, where there is a black range and a table. Page 117 shows how these things are made.

Mary is frying sausages for Alfred. He is very grumpy and hungry and is scolding her for taking so long. He says she is a fool. Mary shuffles about saying, "Oh, dear! Oh, dear!"

The Fire Man sticks his head up through a hole in the range and watches what is happening. He wants to teach the grumpy Alfred a lesson. From below, he pushes the pan with the sausages so that it jumps up and down.

Mary is very surprised, but she calmly puts the pan in its place again. When she turns her back, the Fire Man snatches one of the sausages out of the pan.

Alfred and Mary discover that the sausage has gone. Alfred gets angry and accuses Mary of having eaten it. Mary only says "Oh dear! Oh dear!"

Then they stand guard by the stove. Suddenly they see the Fire Man appear to snatch the other sausage. Furiously, Alfred grabs the Fire Man, but lets him go again quickly, screaming that he has burnt himself.

Alfred walks about moaning, while the Fire Man, with the sausages under his arm, says that Alfred will get his sausages back if he will be kind to his wife. And whenever Alfred is unkind to his wife, the Fire Man will steal his food.

It is hard for Alfred to stop being angry, but he finally manages it. He hugs Mary, who says happily, "Oh dear! Oh dear!"

There are three puppets in the play: Mary, who is timid and afraid, Alfred, her husband, who is grumpy, and the Fire Man, who is an imp living in the kitchen range. Directions for making the puppets are on page 54.

Suppliers

The materials used in this book are available at most art, needlework and department stores. Polystyrene balls are available at some hobby shops and by postal order from some craft suppliers, including:

Needlecraft & Hobbies
83 Northgate
Canterbury
Kent